FREE Study Skills Videos/DVD Offer

Dear Customer,

Thank you for your purchase from Mometrix! We consider it an honor and a privilege that you have purchased our product and we want to ensure your satisfaction.

As a way of showing our appreciation and to help us better serve you, we have developed Study Skills Videos that we would like to give you for FREE. These videos cover our *best practices* for getting ready for your exam, from how to use our study materials to how to best prepare for the day of the test.

All that we ask is that you email us with feedback that would describe your experience so far with our product. Good, bad, or indifferent, we want to know what you think!

To get your FREE Study Skills Videos, you can use the **QR code** below, or send us an **email** at studyvideos@mometrix.com with *FREE VIDEOS* in the subject line and the following information in the body of the email:

- The name of the product you purchased.
- Your product rating on a scale of 1-5, with 5 being the highest rating.
- Your feedback. It can be long, short, or anything in between. We just want to know your impressions and experience so far with our product. (Good feedback might include how our study material met your needs and ways we might be able to make it even better. You could highlight features that you found helpful or features that you think we should add.)

If you have any questions or concerns, please don't hesitate to contact me directly.

Thanks again!

Sincerely,

Jay Willis
Vice President
jay.willis@mometrix.com
1-800-673-8175

US Citizenship Test Study Guide 2021 & 2022

USCIS Naturalization Secrets for Both Exam Versions

Complete Practice Question List

Detailed Answer Explanations

2nd Edition

Written and edited by the Mometrix Adult Education Test Team

Printed in the United States of America

This paper meets the requirements of ANSI/NISO Z39.48-1992 (Permanence of Paper).

Mometrix offers volume discount pricing to institutions. For more information or a price quote, please contact our sales department at sales@mometrix.com or 888-248-1219.

ISBN 13: 978-1-5167-1524-4
ISBN 10: 1-5167-1524-1

DEAR FUTURE EXAM SUCCESS STORY

First of all, **THANK YOU** for purchasing Mometrix study materials!

Second, congratulations! You are one of the few determined test-takers who are committed to doing whatever it takes to excel on your exam. **You have come to the right place.** We developed these study materials with one goal in mind: to deliver you the information you need in a format that's concise and easy to use.

In addition to optimizing your guide for the content of the test, we've outlined our recommended steps for breaking down the preparation process into small, attainable goals so you can make sure you stay on track.

We've also analyzed the entire test-taking process, identifying the most common pitfalls and showing how you can overcome them and be ready for any curveball the test throws you.

Standardized testing is one of the biggest obstacles on your road to success, which only increases the importance of doing well in the high-pressure, high-stakes environment of test day. Your results on this test could have a significant impact on your future, and this guide provides the information and practical advice to help you achieve your full potential on test day.

Your success is our success

We would love to hear from you! If you would like to share the story of your exam success or if you have any questions or comments in regard to our products, please contact us at **800-673-8175** or **support@mometrix.com**.

Thanks again for your business and we wish you continued success!

Sincerely,
The Mometrix Test Preparation Team

TABLE OF CONTENTS

Introduction

Thank you for purchasing this resource! You have made the choice to prepare yourself for a test that could have a huge impact on your future, and this guide is designed to help you be fully ready for test day.

In this guide, we will not only show you **every question** that you might be asked on the test, but we will also give you the background knowledge so you will understand the answers to these questions and why they are important.

If you struggle with **test anxiety**, we strongly encourage you to check out our recommendations for how you can overcome it. Test anxiety is a formidable foe, but it can be beaten, and we want to make sure you have the tools you need to defeat it.

Test Format

There are two parts to the citizenship test: the **English test** and the **civics test**.

The English test will require you to show that you are able to speak, read, and write English well enough to fulfill your duties as a US citizen:

- The interviewer will assess your ability to **speak** English during the eligibility interview.
- To test your **reading** ability, you will be given up to three sentences in English, and you must successfully read aloud at least one of the three sentences in order to pass.
- Similarly, to test your **writing** ability, you will be given up to three sentences in English, and you must successfully write out at least one of the three sentences in order to pass.
- The content of the reading and writing sentences will focus on US history and civics topics.

The civics test will require you to show that you are familiar with the history and the system of government of the United States.

Important Civics Test Update

In 2020, the U.S. Citizenship and Immigration Services amended the civics portion of the naturalization test, with the intent to begin using the new version of the test for all applicants with a filing date (also known as a received date) on or after December 1, 2020. In early 2021, however, the incoming administration made the new version optional until April 19, 2021, and discontinued it entirely after that point. So, unless you are in the very narrow window of applicants who filed after December 1, 2020 and are taking the test before April 19, 2021, you will be taking the **2008 version** of the test.

Filed Pre-December 1, 2020 or Taking Test After April 19, 2021 (2008 Vers.)

- All civics questions are taken from a pool of 100 questions.
- If you are at least 65 years old and have been a US permanent resident for at least 20 years, the question pool for your interview is only 20 questions (those marked with an asterisk '*')
- You will be asked up to 10 questions.
- You must answer at least 6 questions correctly in order to pass.

If you fail to pass one or both sections of the test, you will have another chance to pass the section or sections you failed in a second interview that will take place 60-90 days later.

Some of the content that appears in this guide is taken or adapted from USCIS Form M-638.

FILED POST-DECEMBER 1, 2020 AND TAKING TEST BEFORE APRIL 19, 2021 (2020 VERS.)

- All civics questions are taken from a pool of 128 questions.
- You will be asked up to 20 questions.
- You must answer at least 12 questions correctly in order to pass.
- If you are at least 65 years old and have been a US permanent resident for at least 20 years, the following conditions will apply instead:
  - The question pool is only 20 questions (those marked with an asterisk '*').
  - You will be asked up to 10 questions.
  - You must answer at least 6 questions correctly in order to pass.

If you fail to pass one or both sections of the test, you will have another chance to pass the section or sections you failed in a second interview that will take place 60-90 days later.

Some of the content that appears in this guide is taken or adapted from USCIS Form M-638.

English Test

Reading Test

During your interview, you will be asked to read three sentences so the interviewer can verify that you are able to read English acceptably well. The only words that may be included on these sentences are those in the list below. As you may gather from this list, the sentences will focus on civics and history topics.

People

Abraham Lincoln
George Washington

Civics

American flag
Bill of Rights
capital
citizen
city
Congress
country
Father of Our Country
government
President
right
Senators
state/states
White House

Places

America
United States

U.S. Holidays

Presidents' Day
Memorial Day
Flag Day
Independence Day
Labor Day
Columbus Day
Thanksgiving

Question Words

How
What
When
Where
Who
Why

Verbs

can
come
do/does
elects
have/has
is/are/was/be
lives/lived
meet
name
pay
vote
want

Other (Function)

a
for
here
in
of
on
the
to
we

Other (Content)

colors
dollar bill
first
largest
many
most
north
one
people
second
south

Practice Reading Sentences

Below are some examples of the types of sentences you may be asked to read.

1. A citizen can vote for the President.
2. George Washington was the first President of the United States.
3. We can come here for Independence Day.
4. George Washington is on the one dollar bill.
5. The President lives in the United States capital city.
6. Who elects Senators to Congress?
7. What are the colors of the American flag?
8. We have the right to vote for what we want.
9. Abraham Lincoln lived in the White House.
10. When does Congress meet to vote?
11. We the people have the Bill of Rights.
12. George Washington was the Father of Our Country.
13. The government is of the people and for the people.
14. We come to the city to vote.
15. We meet many people in America.
16. What is the name of the United States President?
17. The state Senators vote for the country.
18. We want to come to the White House for President's Day.
19. The United States is in North America.
20. When can we meet the President?
21. Who are the state Senators?
22. What is the capital city of the United States?
23. Many people lived in the largest city in the country.
24. Where do the people of Congress meet?
25. Most people in the states want to vote.

Writing Test

During your interview, you will also be asked to write three sentences so the interviewer can verify that you are able to write in English acceptably well. Once again, all of the words you may be asked to write are included on the list below. Note that this list is slightly different from the list of words for the reading test.

People

Adams
Lincoln
Washington

Civics

American Indians
capital
citizens
Civil War
Congress
Father of Our Country
flag
free
freedom of speech
President
right
Senators
state/states
White House

Places

Alaska
California
Delaware
Mexico
New York City
United States
Washington
Washington, D.C.

Months

February
May
June
July
September
October
November

Holidays

Presidents' Day
Memorial Day
Flag Day
Independence Day
Labor Day
Columbus Day
Thanksgiving

Verbs

can
come
elect
have/has
is/was/be
lives/lived
meets
pay
vote
want

Other (Function)

and
during
for
here
in
of
on
the
to
we

Other (Content)

blue
dollar bill
fifty/50
first
largest
most
north
one
one hundred/100
people
red
second
south
taxes
white

Practice Writing Sentences

Below are some examples of the types of sentences you may be asked to write. Remember that the interviewer will be reading these sentences to you. You will not get to see them written down, so to best simulate the interview, you should have someone else read these sentences to you so you can practice writing them.

1. President's Day is in February.
2. The White House is in Washington, D.C.
3. The people vote to elect the President.
4. Washington was the Father of our Country.
5. Mexico is south of the United States.
6. Delaware was the first state.
7. Freedom of speech is the right of United States citizens.
8. The President lives in the White House.
9. The United States flag is red, white, and blue.
10. Alaska is the largest state.
11. We elect Senators to Congress.
12. Washington, D.C. is the capital of the United States.
13. The United States has fifty states.
14. Labor Day is in September.
15. United States citizens have the right to vote.
16. The state of California has the most people.
17. Citizens elect the President in November.
18. Congress meets to vote on taxes.
19. Washington is on the one dollar bill.
20. Lincoln lived during the Civil War.
21. Independence Day is in July.
22. Adams was the second President of the United States.
23. Columbus Day is in October.

Civics Questions and Answers (2008 Version)

American Government

In the United States, the government gets its power to govern from the people. We have a government of the people, by the people, and for the people. Citizens in the United States shape their government and its policies, so they must learn about important public issues and get involved in their communities. Learning about American government helps you understand your rights and responsibilities and allows you to fully participate in the American political process. The Founders of this country decided that the United States should be a representative democracy. They wanted a nation ruled by laws, not by men. In a representative democracy, the people choose officials to make laws and represent their views and concerns in government. The following section will help you understand the principles of American democracy, the U.S. system of government, and the important rights and responsibilities of U.S. citizenship.

A. Principles of American Democracy

1. What is the supreme law of the land?

- the Constitution

The Founding Fathers of the United States wrote the Constitution in 1787. The Constitution is the "supreme law of the land." The U.S. Constitution has lasted longer than any other country's constitution. It establishes the basic principles of the United States government. The Constitution establishes a system of government called "representative democracy." In a representative democracy, citizens choose representatives to make the laws. U.S. citizens also choose a president to lead the executive branch of government. The Constitution lists fundamental rights for all citizens and other people living in the United States. Laws made in the United States must follow the Constitution.

2. What does the Constitution do?

- sets up the government
- defines the government
- protects basic rights of Americans

The Constitution of the United States divides government power between the national government and state governments. The name for this division of power is "federalism." Federalism is an important idea in the Constitution. We call the Founding Fathers who wrote the Constitution the "Framers" of the Constitution. The Framers wanted to limit the powers of the government, so they separated the powers into three branches: executive, legislative, and judicial. The Constitution explains the power of each branch. The Constitution also includes changes and additions, called "amendments." The first 10 amendments are called the "Bill of Rights." The Bill of Rights established the individual rights and liberties of all Americans.

3. The idea of self-government is in the first three words of the Constitution. What are these words?

- We the People

The Constitution says:

> "We the People of the United States, in Order to form a more perfect Union, establish Justice, insure domestic Tranquility, provide for the common defence, promote the general Welfare, and secure the Blessings of Liberty to ourselves and our Posterity, do ordain and establish this Constitution for the United States of America."

With the words "We the People," the Constitution states that the people set up the government. The government works for the people and protects the rights of people. In the United States, the power to govern comes from the people, who are the highest power. This is called "popular sovereignty." The people elect representatives to make laws.

4. What is an amendment?

- a change (to the Constitution)
- an addition (to the Constitution)

An amendment is a change or addition to the Constitution. The Framers of the Constitution knew that laws can change as a country grows. They did not want to make it too easy to modify the Constitution, the supreme law of the land. The Framers also did not want the Constitution to lose its meaning. For this reason, the Framers decided that Congress could pass amendments in only two ways: by a two-thirds vote in the U.S. Senate and the House of Representatives or by a special convention. A special convention has to be requested by two-thirds of the states. After an amendment has passed in Congress or by a special convention, the amendment must then be ratified (accepted) by the legislatures of three-fourths of the states. The amendment can also be ratified by a special convention in three-fourths of the states. Not all proposed amendments are ratified. Six times in U.S. history amendments have passed in Congress but were not approved by enough states to be ratified.

5. What do we call the first ten amendments to the Constitution?

- the Bill of Rights

The Bill of Rights is the first 10 amendments to the Constitution. When the Framers wrote the Constitution, they did not focus on individual rights. They focused on creating the system and structure of government. Many Americans believed that the Constitution should guarantee the rights of the people, and they wanted a list of all the things a government could not do. They were afraid that a strong government would take away the rights people won in the Revolutionary War. James Madison, one of the Framers of the

Constitution, wrote a list of individual rights and limits on the government. These rights appear in the first 10 amendments, called the Bill of Rights. Some of these rights include freedom of expression, the right to bear arms, freedom from search without warrant, freedom not to be tried twice for the same crime, the right to not testify against yourself, the right to a trial by a jury of your peers, the right to an attorney, and protection against excessive fines and unusual punishments. The Bill of Rights was ratified in 1791.

6. What is one right or freedom from the First Amendment?

- speech
- religion
- assembly
- press
- petition the government

The First Amendment of the Bill of Rights protects a person's right to freedom of expression. Freedom of expression allows open discussion and debate on public issues. Open discussion and debate are important to democracy. The First Amendment also protects freedom of religion and free speech. This amendment says that Congress may not pass laws that establish an official religion and may not limit religious expression. Congress may not pass laws that limit freedom of the press or the right of people to meet peacefully. The First Amendment also gives people the right to petition the government to change laws or acts that are not fair. Congress may not take away these rights. The First Amendment of the Constitution guarantees and protects these rights.

7. How many amendments does the Constitution have?

- twenty-seven (27)

The first 10 amendments to the Constitution are called the Bill of Rights. They were added in 1791. Since then, 17 more amendments have been added. The Constitution currently has 27 amendments. The 27th Amendment was added in 1992. It explains how senators and representatives are paid. Interestingly, Congress first discussed this amendment back in 1789 as one of the original amendments considered for the Bill of Rights.

8. What did the Declaration of Independence do?

- announced our independence (from Great Britain)
- declared our independence (from Great Britain)
- said that the United States is free (from Great Britain)

The Declaration of Independence contains important ideas about the American system of government. The Declaration of Independence states that all people are created equal and have "certain unalienable rights." These are rights that no government can change or take away. The author of the Declaration, Thomas Jefferson, wrote that the American colonies should be independent because Great Britain did not respect the basic rights of people in the colonies. Jefferson believed that a government exists only if the people think it should. He believed in the idea that the people create their own government and consent, or agree, to follow laws their government makes. This idea is called "consent of the governed." If the government creates laws that are fair and protect people, then people will agree to follow those laws. In the Declaration of Independence, Jefferson wrote a list of complaints the colonists had against the King of England. Jefferson ended the Declaration with the statement that the colonies are, and should be, free and independent states. The Second Continental Congress voted to accept the Declaration on July 4, 1776.

9. What are two rights in the Declaration of Independence?

- life
- liberty
- pursuit of happiness

The Declaration of Independence lists three rights that the Founding Fathers considered to be natural and "unalienable." They are the right to life, liberty, and the pursuit of happiness. These ideas about freedom and individual rights were the basis for declaring America's independence. Thomas Jefferson and the other Founding Fathers believed that people are born with natural rights that no government can take away. Government exists to protect these rights. Because the people voluntarily give up power to a government, they can take that power back. The British government was not protecting the rights of the colonists, so the colonies took back their power and separated from Great Britain.

10. What is freedom of religion?

- You can practice any religion, or not practice a religion.

Colonists from Spain, France, Holland, England, and other countries came to America for many different reasons. One of the reasons was religious freedom. The rulers of many of these countries told their citizens that they must go to a certain church and worship in a certain way. Some people had different religious beliefs than their rulers and wanted to have their own churches. In 1620, the Pilgrims were the first group that came to America seeking religious freedom. Religious freedom was also important to the Framers. For this reason, freedom of religion was included in the Constitution as part of the Bill of Rights. The First Amendment to the Constitution guarantees freedom of religion. The First Amendment states, "Congress shall make no law respecting an establishment of religion, or prohibiting the free exercise thereof." The First Amendment also prohibits Congress from setting up an official U.S. religion, and protects citizens' rights to hold any religious belief, or none at all.

11. What is the economic system in the United States?*

- capitalist economy
- market economy

The economic system of the United States is capitalism. In the American economy, most businesses are privately owned. Competition and profit motivate businesses. Businesses and consumers interact in the marketplace, where prices can be negotiated.

called a "market economy." In a market economy, businesses decide what to produce, how much to produce, and what to charge. Consumers decide what, when, and where they will buy goods or services. In a market economy, competition, supply, and demand influence the decisions of businesses and consumers.

12. What is the "rule of law"?

- Everyone must follow the law.
- Leaders must obey the law.
- Government must obey the law.
- No one is above the law.

John Adams was one of the Founding Fathers and the second president of the United States. He wrote that our country is, "a government of laws, and not of men." No person or group is above the law. The rule of law means that everyone (citizens and leaders) must obey the laws. In the United States, the U.S. Constitution is the foundation for the rule of law. The United States is a "constitutional democracy" (a democracy with a constitution). In constitutional democracies, people are willing to obey the laws because the laws are made by the people through their elected representatives. If all people are governed by the same laws, the individual rights and liberties of each person are better protected. The rule of law helps to make sure that government protects all people equally and does not violate the rights of certain people.

B: System of Government

13. Name one branch or part of the government.*

- Congress
- legislative
- President
- executive
- the courts
- judicial

The Constitution establishes three branches of government: legislative, executive, and judicial. Article I of the Constitution establishes the legislative branch. Article I explains that Congress makes laws. Congress (the Senate and the House of Representatives) is the legislative branch of the U.S. government. Article II of the Constitution establishes the executive branch. The executive branch enforces the laws that Congress passes. The executive branch makes sure all the people follow the laws of the United States. The president is the head of the executive branch. The vice president and members of the president's cabinet are also part of the executive branch. Article III of the Constitution establishes the judicial branch. The judicial branch places the highest judicial power in the Supreme Court. One responsibility of the judicial branch is to decide if government laws and actions follow the Constitution. This is a very important responsibility.

14. What stops one branch of government from becoming too powerful?

- checks and balances
- separation of powers

The Constitution separates the government's power into three branches to prevent one person or group from having too much power. The separation of government into three branches creates a system of checks and balances. This means that each branch can block, or threaten to block, the actions of the other branches. Here are some examples: the Senate (part of the legislative branch) can block a treaty signed by the president (the executive branch). In this example, the legislative branch is "checking" the executive. The U.S. Supreme Court (the judicial branch) can reject a law passed by Congress (the legislative branch). In this example, the judicial branch is "checking" the legislative branch. This separation of powers limits the power of the government and prevents the government from violating the rights of the people.

15. Who is in charge of the executive branch?

- the President

The job of the executive branch is to carry out, or execute, federal laws and enforce laws passed by Congress. The head of the executive branch is the president. The president is both the head of state and the head of government. The president's powers include the ability to sign treaties with other countries and to select ambassadors to represent the United States around the world. The president also sets national policies and proposes laws to Congress. The president names the top leaders of the federal departments. When there is a vacancy on the Supreme Court, the president names a new member. However, the Senate has the power to reject the president's choices. This limit on the power of the president is an example of checks and balances.

16. Who makes federal laws?

- Congress
- Senate and House (of Representatives)
- (U.S. or national) legislature

Congress makes federal laws. A federal law usually applies to all states and all people in the United States. Either side of Congress—the Senate or the House of Representatives—can propose a bill to address an issue. When the Senate proposes a bill, it sends the bill to a Senate committee. The Senate committee studies the issue and the bill. When the House of Representatives proposes a bill, it sends the bill to a House of Representatives committee. The committee studies the bill and sometimes makes changes to it. Then the bill goes to the full House or Senate for consideration. When each chamber passes its own version of the bill, it often goes to a "conference committee." The conference committee has members from both the House and the Senate. This committee discusses the bill, tries to resolve the differences, and writes a report with the final version of the bill. Then the committee sends the final version of the bill back to both houses for approval. If both houses approve the bill, it is considered "enrolled." An enrolled bill goes to the president to be signed into law. If the president signs the bill, it becomes a federal law.

17. What are the two parts of the U.S. Congress?*

- the Senate and House (of Representatives)

Congress is divided into two parts—the Senate and the House of Representatives. Because it has two "chambers," the U.S. Congress is known as a "bicameral" legislature. The system of checks and balances works in Congress. Specific powers are assigned to each of these chambers. For example, only the Senate has the power to reject a treaty signed by the president or a person the president chooses to serve on the Supreme Court. Only the House of Representatives has the power to introduce a bill that requires Americans to pay taxes.

18. How many U.S. Senators are there?

- one hundred (100)

There are 100 senators in Congress, two from each state. All states have equal power in the Senate because each state has the same number of senators. States with a very small population have the same number of senators as states with very large populations. The Framers of the Constitution made sure that the Senate would be small. This would keep it more orderly than the larger House of Representatives. As James Madison wrote in Federalist Paper #63, the Senate should be a "temperate and respectable body of citizens" that operates in a "cool and deliberate" way.

19. We elect a U.S. Senator for how many years?

- six (6)

The Framers of the Constitution wanted senators to be independent from public opinion. They thought a fairly long, six-year term would give them this protection. They also wanted longer Senate terms to balance the shorter two-year terms of the members of the House, who would more closely follow public opinion. The Constitution puts no limit on the number of terms a senator may serve. Elections for U.S. senators take place on even-numbered years. Every two years, one-third of the senators are up for election.

20. Who is one of your state's U.S. Senators now?*

- Answers will vary. [District of Columbia residents and residents of U.S. territories should answer that D.C. (or the territory where the applicant lives) has no U.S. Senators.]

For a complete list of U.S. senators and the states they represent, go to: www.senate.gov.

21. The House of Representatives has how many voting members?

- four hundred thirty-five (435)

The House of Representatives is the larger chamber of Congress. Since 1912, the House of Representatives has had 435 voting members. However, the distribution of members among the states has changed over the years. Each state must have at least one representative in the House. Beyond that, the number of representatives from each state depends on the population of the state. The Constitution says that the government will conduct a census of the population every 10 years to count the number of people in each state. The results of the census are used to recalculate the number of representatives each state should have. For example, if one state gains many residents that state could get one or more new representatives. If another state loses residents, that state could lose one or more. But the total number of voting U.S. representatives does not change.

22. We elect a U.S. Representative for how many years?

- two (2)

People who live in a representative's district are called "constituents." Representatives tend to reflect the views of their constituents. If representatives do not do this, they may be voted out of office. The Framers of the Constitution believed that short two-year terms and frequent elections would keep representatives close to their constituents, public opinion, and more aware of local and community concerns. The Constitution puts no limit on the number of terms a representative may serve. All representatives are up for election every two years.

23. Name your U.S. Representative.

- Answers will vary. [Residents of territories with nonvoting Delegates or Resident Commissioners may provide the name of that Delegate or Commissioner. Also acceptable is any statement that the territory has no (voting) Representatives in Congress.]

For a complete list of U.S. representatives and the districts they represent, go to: www.house.gov.

24. Who does a U.S. Senator represent?

- all people of the state

Senators are elected to serve the people of their state for six years. Each of the two senators represents the entire state. Before the 17th Amendment to the Constitution was ratified in 1913, the state legislatures elected the U.S. senators to represent their state. Now, all the voters in a state elect their two U.S. senators directly.

25. Why do some states have more Representatives than other states?

- (because of) the state's population
- (because) they have more people
- (because) some states have more people

The Founding Fathers wanted people in all states to be represented fairly. In the House of Representatives, a state's population determines the number of representatives it has. In this way, states with many people have a stronger voice in the House. In the Senate, every state has the same number of senators. This means that states with few people still have a strong voice in the national government.

26. We elect a President for how many years?

- four (4)

Early American leaders thought that the head of the British government, the king, had too much power. Because of this, they limited the powers of the head of the new U.S. government. They decided that the people would elect the president every four years.

The president is the only official elected by the entire country through the Electoral College. The Electoral College is a process that was designed by the writers of the Constitution to select presidents. It came from a compromise between the president being elected directly by the people and the president being chosen by Congress. Citizens vote for electors, who then choose the president. Before 1951, there was no limit on the number of terms a president could serve. With the 22nd Amendment to the Constitution, the president can only be elected to two terms (four years each) for a total of eight years.

27. In what month do we vote for President?*

- November

The Constitution did not set a national election day. In the past, elections for federal office took place on different days in different states. In 1845, Congress passed legislation to designate a single day for all Americans to vote. It made Election Day the Tuesday after the first Monday in November. Congress chose November because the United States was mostly rural. By November, farmers had completed their harvests and were available to vote. Another reason for this date was the weather. People were able to travel because it was not yet winter. They chose Tuesday for Election Day so that voters had a full day after Sunday to travel to the polls.

28. What is the name of the President of the United States now?*

- Joseph R. Biden, Jr.
- Joe Biden
- Biden

Joe Biden is the 46th president of the United States. As president he is the head of the executive branch. As commander in chief, he is also in charge of the military. Biden was

Vice President from 2009 to 2017 under President Barack Obama. Prior to becoming vice president, Biden served in the U.S. Senate for 36 years. President Biden's wife, called "the First Lady," is Jill Biden.

29. What is the name of the Vice President of the United States now?

- Kamala D. Harris
- Kamala Harris
- Harris

Kamala Harris is the 49th vice president of the United States. She graduated from Howard University. She also earned her law degree from the University of California, Hastings. Prior to becoming vice president, Harris served 4 years in the U.S. Senate, 6 years as Attorney General of California, and 7 years as District Attorney of San Francisco. As vice president, Harris is president of the U.S. Senate and a top advisor to the president. Vice President Harris is married to Doug Emhoff.

30. If the President can no longer serve, who becomes President?

- the Vice President

If the president dies, resigns, or cannot work while still in office, the vice president becomes president. For this reason, the qualifications for vice president and president are the same. A vice president became president nine times in U.S. history when the president died or left office. William Henry Harrison died in office in 1841. Zachary Taylor died in office in 1850. Abraham Lincoln was killed in office in 1865. James Garfield was killed in office in 1881. William McKinley was killed in office in 1901. Warren Harding died in office in 1923. Franklin Roosevelt died in office in 1945. John F. Kennedy was killed in office in 1963. Richard Nixon resigned from office in 1974. No one other than the vice president has ever succeeded to the presidency.

31. If both the President and the Vice President can no longer serve, who becomes President?

- the Speaker of the House

If both the president and vice president cannot serve, the next person in line is the speaker of the House of Representatives. This has not always been the procedure. Soon after the country was founded, a law was passed that made the Senate president pro tempore the next in line after the president and vice president. The president pro tempore presides over the Senate when the vice president is not there. Later in U.S. history, the secretary of state was third in line. With the Presidential Succession Act of 1947, Congress returned to the original idea of having a congressional leader next in line. In 1967, the 25th Amendment was ratified. It established procedures for presidential and vice-presidential succession.

32. Who is the Commander in Chief of the military?

- the President

The Founding Fathers strongly believed in republican ideals. A republic is a government where a country's political power comes from the citizens, not the rulers, and is put into use by representatives elected by the citizens. That is why they made the president the commander in chief. They wanted a civilian selected by the people. They did not want a professional military leader. The president commands the armed forces, but Congress has the power to pay for the armed forces and declare war. In 1973, many members of Congress believed that the president was misusing or abusing his powers as commander in chief. They thought that the president was ignoring the legislative branch and not allowing the system of checks and balances to work. In response, Congress passed the War Powers Act. The War Powers Act gave Congress a stronger voice in decisions about the use of U.S. troops. President Richard Nixon vetoed this bill, but Congress overrode his veto. Because we have a system of checks and balances, one branch of government is able to check the other branches.

33. Who signs bills to become laws?

- the President

Every law begins as a proposal made by a member of Congress, either a senator (member of the Senate) or representative (member of the House of Representatives). When the Senate or House begins to debate the proposal, it is called a "bill." After debate in both houses of Congress, if a majority of both the Senate and House vote to pass the bill, it goes to the president. If the president wants the bill to become law, he signs it. If the president does not want the bill to become law, he vetoes it. The president cannot introduce a bill. If he has an idea for a bill, he must ask a member of Congress to introduce it.

34. Who vetoes bills?

- the President

The president has veto power. This means that the president can reject a bill passed by Congress. If the president vetoes a bill, he prevents it from becoming a law. The president can send the bill back to Congress unsigned. Often, he will list reasons why he rejects it. The president has 10 days to evaluate the bill. If the president does not sign the bill after 10 days and Congress is in session, the bill automatically becomes a law. If the president does nothing with the bill and Congress adjourns within the 10-day period, the bill does not become law—this is called a "pocket veto." If two-thirds of the House and two-thirds of the Senate vote to pass the bill again, the bill becomes a law, even though the president did not sign it. This process is called "overriding the president's veto." It is not easy to do.

35. What does the President's Cabinet do?

- advises the President

The Constitution says that the leaders of the executive departments should advise the president. These department leaders, most of them called "secretaries," make up the cabinet. The president nominates the cabinet members to be his advisors. For a nominee to be confirmed, a majority of the Senate must approve the nominee. Throughout history, presidents have been able to change who makes up the cabinet or add departments to the cabinet. For example, when the Department of Homeland Security was created, President George W. Bush added the leader of this department to his cabinet.

36. What are two Cabinet-level positions?

Attorney General
Vice President

Secretary of Agriculture
Secretary of Commerce
Secretary of Defense
Secretary of Education
Secretary of Energy
Secretary of Health and Human Services
Secretary of Homeland Security
Secretary of Housing and Urban Development
Secretary of the Interior
Secretary of Labor
Secretary of State
Secretary of Transportation
Secretary of the Treasury
Secretary of Veterans Affairs

The people on the president's cabinet are the vice president and the heads of the 15 executive departments. The president may appoint other government officials to the cabinet. When George Washington was president, there were only four cabinet members: the secretary of state, secretary of the treasury, secretary of war, and attorney general. The government established the other executive departments later.

37. What does the judicial branch do?

- reviews laws
- explains laws
- resolves disputes (disagreements)
- decides if a law goes against the Constitution

The judicial branch is one of the three branches of government. The Constitution established the judicial branch of government with the creation of the Supreme Court. Congress created the other federal courts. All these courts together make up the judicial branch. The courts review and explain the laws, and they resolve disagreements about the meaning of the law. The U.S. Supreme Court makes sure that laws are consistent with the Constitution. If a law is not consistent with the Constitution, the Court can declare it unconstitutional. In this case, the Court rejects the law. The Supreme Court makes the final decision about all cases that have to do with federal laws and treaties. It also rules on other cases, such as disagreements between states.

38. What is the highest court in the United States?

- the Supreme Court

The U.S. Supreme Court has complete authority over all federal courts. Its rulings have a significant effect. A Supreme Court ruling can affect the outcome of many cases in the lower courts. The Supreme Court's interpretations of federal laws and of the Constitution are final. The Supreme Court is limited in its power over the states. It cannot make decisions about state law or state constitutions. The Court can decide that a state law or action conflicts with federal law or with the U.S. Constitution. If this happens, the state law becomes invalid. The Supreme Court case ruling Marbury v. Madison established this power, known as "judicial review." The Supreme Court also rules on cases about significant social and public policy issues that affect all Americans. The Supreme Court ruled on the court case Brown v. the Board of Education of Topeka, which ended racial segregation in schools.

39. How many justices are on the Supreme Court?

- nine (9)

The Constitution does not establish the number of justices on the Supreme Court. In the past, there have been as many as 10 and as few as six justices. Now, there are nine justices on the Supreme Court: eight associate justices and one chief justice. The Constitution gives the president the power to nominate justices to the Supreme Court. The nominee must then be confirmed by the Senate. Justices serve on the court for life or until they retire. For more information on the Supreme Court, go to www.supremecourt.gov.

40. Who is the Chief Justice of the United States now?

- John Roberts (John G. Roberts, Jr.)

John G. Roberts, Jr. is the 17th chief justice of the United States. After the death of former chief justice William Rehnquist in September 2005, President George W. Bush nominated Roberts for this position. Judge Roberts became chief justice when he was 50. He is the youngest chief justice since 1801, when John Marshall became chief justice at the age of 45. Before he became chief justice, Judge Roberts served on the U.S. Court of Appeals for the District of Columbia Circuit. Although the chief justice of the United States is the highest official in the judicial branch, his vote on the Supreme Court carries the same weight as the other justices.

41. Under our Constitution, some powers belong to the federal government. What is one power of the federal government?

- to print money
- to declare war
- to create an army
- to make treaties

The powers of government are divided between the federal government and the state governments. The federal government is known as a limited government. Its powers are restricted to those described in the U.S. Constitution. The Constitution gives the federal government the power to print money, declare war, create an army, and make treaties with other nations. Most other powers that are not given to the federal government in the Constitution belong to the states.

42. Under our Constitution, some powers belong to the states. What is one power of the states?

- provide schooling and education
- provide protection (police)
- provide safety (fire departments)
- give a driver's license
- approve zoning and land use

In the United States, the federal and state governments both hold power. Before the Constitution, the 13 colonies governed themselves individually much like state governments. It was not until the Articles of Confederation and then the Constitution that a national or federal government was established. Today, although each state has its own constitution, these state constitutions cannot conflict with the U.S. Constitution. The U.S. Constitution is the supreme law of the land. The state governments hold powers not given to the federal government in the U.S. Constitution. Some powers of the state government are the power to create traffic regulations and marriage requirements, and to issue driver's licenses. The Constitution also provides a list of powers that the states do not have. For example, states cannot coin (create) money. The state and federal governments also share some powers, such as the ability to tax people.

43. Who is the Governor of your state now?

- Answers will vary. [District of Columbia residents should answer that D.C. does not have a Governor.]

To learn the name of the governor of your state or territory, go to: www.nga.org/governors.

Similar to the federal government, most states have three branches of government. The branches are executive, legislative, and judicial. The governor is the chief executive of the state. The governor's job in a state government is similar to the president's job in the federal government. However, the state laws that a governor carries out are different from the federal laws that the president carries out. The Constitution says that certain issues are covered by federal, not state, laws. All other issues are covered by state laws. The governor's duties and powers vary from state to state. The number of years that a governor is elected to serve—called a "term"—is four years. The exceptions are New Hampshire and Vermont, where governors serve for two years.

44. What is the capital of your state?*

- Answers will vary. [District of Columbia residents should answer that D.C. is not a state and does not have a capital. Residents of U.S. territories should name the capital of the territory.]

To learn the capital of your state or territory, go to: www.census.gov/schools/facts.

Each state or territory has its own capital. The state capital is where the state government conducts its business. It is similar to the nation's capital, Washington, D.C., where the federal government conducts its business. Some state capitals have moved from one city to another over the years, but the state capitals have not changed since 1910. Usually, the governor lives in the state's capital city.

45. What are the two major political parties in the United States?*

- Democratic and Republican

The Constitution did not establish political parties. President George Washington specifically warned against them. But early in U.S. history, two political groups developed. They were the Democratic-Republicans and the Federalists. Today, the two major political parties are the Democratic Party and the Republican Party. President Andrew Jackson created the Democratic Party from the Democratic-Republicans. The Republican Party took over from the Whigs as a major party in the 1860s. The first Republican president was Abraham Lincoln. Throughout U.S. history, there have been other parties. These parties have included the Know-Nothing (also called American Party), Bull-Moose (also called Progressive), Reform, and Green parties. They have played various roles in American politics. Political party membership in the United States is voluntary. Parties are made up of people who organize to promote their candidates for election and to promote their views about public policies.

46. What is the political party of the President now?

- Democratic (Party)

The two major political parties in the United States today are the Democratic and Republican parties. Notable Republican presidents include Abraham Lincoln, Theodore Roosevelt, Warren Harding, Herbert Hoover, Dwight Eisenhower, Ronald Reagan, George H. W. Bush, and George W. Bush. Notable Democratic presidents include Woodrow Wilson, Franklin D. Roosevelt, Harry Truman, John F. Kennedy, Lyndon B. Johnson, Jimmy Carter, William "Bill" Clinton, and Barack Obama. Since the middle of the 19th century, the symbol of the Republican Party has been the elephant. The Republican Party is also known as the "Grand Old Party" or the "GOP." The symbol of the Democratic Party is the donkey.

47. What is the name of the Speaker of the House of Representatives now?

- Nancy Pelosi
- Pelosi

The current Speaker of the House of Representatives is Nancy Pelosi. She has represented California's Twelfth Congressional District (as well as the Fifth and Eighth Districts, due to redrawn district boundaries) in the House of Representatives since 1987. As speaker, she presides over the House of Representatives and leads the majority political party in the House, the Democratic Party. The speaker is second in line to the succession of the presidency after the vice president.

C: Rights and Responsibilities

48. There are four amendments to the Constitution about who can vote. Describe one of them.

- Citizens eighteen (18) and older (can vote).
- You don't have to pay (a poll tax) to vote.
- Any citizen can vote. (Women and men can vote.)
- A male citizen of any race (can vote).

Voting is one of the most important civic responsibilities of citizens in the United States. In a democratic society, the people choose the leaders who will represent them. There are four amendments to the Constitution about voting. The 15th Amendment permits American men of all races to vote. It was written after the Civil War and the end of slavery. The 19th Amendment gave women the right to vote. It resulted from the women's suffrage movement (the women's rights movement). After the 15th Amendment was passed, some leaders of the southern states were upset that African Americans could vote. These leaders designed fees called poll taxes to stop them from voting. The 24th Amendment made these poll taxes illegal. The 26th Amendment lowered the voting age from 21 to 18.

49. What is one responsibility that is only for United States citizens?*

- serve on a jury
- vote in a federal election

Two responsibilities of U.S. citizens are to serve on a jury and vote in federal elections. The Constitution gives citizens the right to a trial by a jury. The jury is made up of U.S. citizens. Participation of citizens on a jury helps ensure a fair trial. Another important responsibility of citizens is voting. The law does not require citizens to vote, but voting is a very important part of any democracy. By voting, citizens are participating in the democratic process. Citizens vote for leaders to represent them and their ideas, and the leaders support the citizens' interests.

50. Name one right only for United States citizens.

- vote in a federal election
- run for federal office

U.S. citizens have the right to vote in federal elections. Permanent residents can vote in local or state elections that do not require voters to be U.S. citizens. Only U.S. citizens can vote in federal elections. U.S. citizens can also run for federal office. Qualifications to run for the Senate or House of Representatives include being a U.S. citizen for a certain number of years. A candidate for Senate must be a U.S. citizen for at least 9 years. A candidate for the House must be a U.S. citizen for at least 7 years. To run for president of the United States, a candidate must be a native-born (not naturalized) citizen. In addition to the benefits of citizenship, U.S. citizens have certain responsibilities—to respect the law, stay informed on issues, participate in the democratic process, and pay their taxes.

51. What are two rights of everyone living in the United States?

- freedom of expression
- freedom of speech
- freedom of assembly
- freedom to petition the government
- freedom of religion
- the right to bear arms

Thomas Jefferson said, "[The] best principles [of our republic] secure to all its citizens a perfect equality of rights." Millions of immigrants have come to America to have these rights. The Constitution and the Bill of Rights give many of these rights to all people living in the United States. These rights include the freedom of expression, of religion, of speech, and the right to bear arms. All people living in the United States also have many of the same duties as citizens, such as paying taxes and obeying the laws.

52. What do we show loyalty to when we say the Pledge of Allegiance?

- the United States
- the flag

The flag is an important symbol of the United States. The Pledge of Allegiance to the flag states, "I pledge allegiance to the Flag of the United States of America, and to the Republic for which it stands, one Nation under God, indivisible, with liberty and justice for all." When we say the Pledge of Allegiance, we usually stand facing the flag with the right hand over the heart. Francis Bellamy wrote the pledge. It was first published in The Youth's Companion magazine in 1892 for children to say on the anniversary of Columbus's discovery of America. Congress officially recognized the pledge on June 22, 1942. Two changes have been made since it was written in 1892. "I pledge allegiance to my flag" was changed to "I pledge allegiance to the Flag of the United States of America." Congress added the phrase "under God" on June 14, 1954.

53. What is one promise you make when you become a United States citizen?

- give up loyalty to other countries
- defend the Constitution and laws of the United States
- obey the laws of the United States
- serve in the U.S. military (if needed)
- serve (do important work for) the nation (if needed)
- be loyal to the United States

When the United States became an independent country, the Constitution gave Congress the power to establish a uniform rule of naturalization. Congress made rules about how immigrants could become citizens. Many of these requirements are still valid today, such as the requirements to live in the United States for a specific period of time, to be of good moral character, and to understand and support the principles of the Constitution. After an immigrant fulfills all of the requirements to become a U.S. citizen, the final step is to take an Oath of Allegiance at a naturalization ceremony.

The Oath of Allegiance states, "I hereby declare, on oath, that I absolutely and entirely renounce and abjure all allegiance and fidelity to any foreign prince, potentate, state, or sovereignty of whom or which I have heretofore been a subject or citizen; that I will support and defend the Constitution and laws of the United States of America against all enemies, foreign and domestic; that I will bear true faith and allegiance to the same; that I will bear arms on behalf of the United States when required by the law; that I will perform noncombatant service in the Armed Forces of the United States when required by the law; that I will perform work of national importance under civilian direction when required by the law; and that I take this obligation freely without any mental reservation or purpose of evasion; so help me God."

54. How old do citizens have to be to vote for President?*

- eighteen (18) and older

For most of U.S. history, Americans had to be at least 21 years old to vote. At the time of the Vietnam War, during the 1960s and 1970s, many people thought that people who were old enough to fight in a war should also be old enough to vote. In 1971, the 26th Amendment changed the minimum voting age from 21 to 18 for all federal, state, and local elections. The National Voter Registration Act of 1993 made it easier for people to register to vote. Now they can register to vote by mail, at public assistance offices, or when they apply for or renew their driver's license.

55. What are two ways that Americans can participate in their democracy?

vote
join a political party
help with a campaign
join a civic group
join a community group
give an elected official your opinion on an issue
call Senators and Representatives
publicly support or oppose an issue or policy
run for office
write to a newspaper
call Senators and Representatives

Citizens play an active part in their communities. When Americans engage in the political process, democracy stays alive and strong. There are many ways for people to be involved. They can volunteer to help new immigrants learn English and civics, join the Parent Teacher Association (PTA) of their child's school, run for a position on the local school board, or volunteer to help at a polling station. People can also vote, help with a political campaign, join a civic or community organization, or call their senator or representative about an issue that is important to them.

56. When is the last day you can send in federal income tax forms?*

- April 15

The last day to send in your federal income tax to the Internal Revenue Service is April 15 of each year. The Constitution gave the federal government the power to collect taxes. The federal government needs money to pay the nation's debts and to defend and provide for the needs of the country. When the country was young, it was difficult to raise money from the 13 original states. The government began collecting income tax for the first time through the Revenue Act of 1861. This was only temporary. In 1894, a flat-rate federal income tax was enacted, but the Supreme Court said this was unconstitutional. Finally, in 1913, the 16th Amendment was ratified. It gave Congress the power to collect income taxes. Today, "taxable income" is money that is earned from wages, self-employment, tips, and the sale of property. The government uses these taxes to keep our country safe and secure. It also tries to cure and prevent diseases through research. In addition, the government uses these taxes to educate children and adults, and build and repair our roads and highways. Taxes are used to do these things and many more.

57. When must all men register for the Selective Service?

- at age eighteen (18)
- between eighteen (18) and twenty-six (26)

President Lincoln tried to draft men to fight during the Civil War, but many people became angry and rioted. In 1917, Congress passed the Selective Service Act. This act gave President Woodrow Wilson the power to temporarily increase the U.S. military during World War I. In 1940, President Franklin Roosevelt signed the Selective Training and Service Act, which created the first draft during peacetime. This was the beginning of the Selective Service System in the United States today. The draft was needed again for the Korean and Vietnam Wars. Today, there is no draft, but all men between 18 and 26 years old must register with the Selective Service System. When a man registers, he tells the government that he is available to serve in the U.S. Armed Forces. He can register at a United States post office or on the Internet. To register for Selective Service on the Internet, visit the Selective Service website at: www.sss.gov.

American History

For more than 200 years, the United States has strived to become a "more perfect union." Its history has been one of expansive citizenship for all Americans. By learning about our shared history, you will be able to understand our nation's traditions, milestones, and common civic values. Our country is independent because of the strength, unity, and determination of our forefathers. It is important for future Americans to know this story. We are people working toward great ideals and principles guided by equality and fairness. This is important to keep our country free. As Americans, we have been committed to each other and our country throughout our history. The following section will help you understand American history from the colonial period and independence to the Civil War and other important events during the 1800s, 1900s, and today.

A: Colonial Period and Independence

58. What is one reason colonists came to America?

- freedom
- political liberty
- religious freedom
- economic opportunity
- practice their religion
- escape persecution

In the 1600s and 1700s, colonists from England and other European countries sailed across the Atlantic Ocean to the American colonies. Some left Europe to escape religious restrictions or persecution, to practice their religion freely. Many came for political freedom, and some came for economic opportunity. These freedoms and opportunities often did not exist in the colonists' home countries. For these settlers, the American colonies were a chance for freedom and a new life. Today, many people come to the United States for these same reasons.

59. Who lived in America before the Europeans arrived?

- American Indians
- Native Americans

Great American Indian tribes such as the Navajo, Sioux, Cherokee, and Iroquois lived in America at the time the Pilgrims arrived. The Pilgrims settled in an area where a tribe called the Wampanoag lived. The Wampanoag taught the Pilgrims important skills, such as how to farm with different methods and how to grow crops such as corn, beans, and squash. Relations with some American Indian tribes became tense and confrontational as more Europeans moved to America and migrated west. Eventually, after much violence, the settlers defeated those American Indian tribes and took much of their land.

60. What group of people was taken to America and sold as slaves?

- Africans
- people from Africa

Slavery existed in many countries long before America was founded. By 1700, many Africans were being brought to the American colonies as slaves. Men, women, and children were brought against their will. They were often separated from their families when they were sold as slaves. Slaves worked without payment and without basic rights. Most worked in agriculture, but slaves did many other kinds of work in the colonies, too. Slavery created a challenge for a nation founded on individual freedoms and democratic beliefs. It was one of the major causes of the American Civil War.

61. Why did the colonists fight the British?

- because of high taxes (taxation without representation)
- because the British army stayed in their houses (boarding, quartering)
- because they didn't have self-government

The American colonists' anger had been growing for years before the Revolutionary War began in 1775. The decision to separate from the British was not an easy choice for many colonists. However, Great Britain's "repeated injuries" against the Americans, as noted in the Declaration of Independence, convinced many to join the rebellion. The British taxed the colonists without their consent, and the colonists had nobody to represent their needs and ideas to the British government. They were also angry because ordinary colonists were forced to let British soldiers sleep and eat in their homes. The colonists believed the British did not respect their basic rights. The British governed the colonists without their consent, denying them self-government.

62. Who wrote the Declaration of Independence?

- (Thomas) Jefferson

Thomas Jefferson wrote the Declaration of Independence in 1776. He was a very important political leader and thinker. Some of the most important ideas about the American government are found in the Declaration of Independence, such as the idea that all people are created equal. Another important idea is that people are born with certain rights including life, liberty, and the pursuit of happiness. Jefferson was the third president of the United States, serving from 1801 to 1809. Before becoming president, Jefferson was governor of Virginia and the first U.S. secretary of state. He strongly supported individual rights, especially freedom of religion. Jefferson wanted to protect these rights. For this reason, he did not want a strong national government.

63. When was the Declaration of Independence adopted?

- July 4, 1776

In 1774, representatives from 12 of the 13 colonies met in Philadelphia, Pennsylvania, for the First Continental Congress. Of the 13 colonies, only Georgia was absent. These representatives were angry about British laws that treated them unfairly. They began to organize an army. The Second Continental Congress met in 1775 after fighting began between the colonists and the British Army. This Congress asked Thomas Jefferson and others to write the Declaration of Independence. When Thomas Jefferson finished his draft of the Declaration of Independence, he took it to John Adams, Benjamin Franklin, and the others on the committee to review it. After changes were made by the committee, the Declaration was read to the members of the entire Congress. The purpose of the Declaration was to announce the separation of the colonies from England. The Declaration of Independence stated that if a government does not protect the rights of the people, the people can create a new government. For this reason, the colonists separated from their British rulers. On July 4, 1776, the Second Continental Congress adopted the Declaration of Independence.

64. There were 13 original states. Name three.

New Hampshire
Delaware
Massachusetts
Maryland
Rhode Island
Virginia
Connecticut
North Carolina
New York
South Carolina
New Jersey
Georgia
Pennsylvania

The 13 original states were all former British colonies. Representatives from these colonies came together and declared independence from Great Britain in 1776. After the Revolutionary War, the colonies became free and independent states. When the 13 colonies became states, each state set up its own government. They wrote state constitutions. Eventually, the people in these states created a new form of national government that would unite all the states into a single nation under the U.S. Constitution. The first three colonies to become states were Delaware, Pennsylvania, and New Jersey. This happened in 1787. Eight colonies became states in 1788. These were Georgia, Connecticut, Massachusetts, Maryland, South Carolina, New Hampshire, Virginia, and New York. North Carolina became a state in 1789. Rhode Island became a state in 1790. Although the colonies were recognized as states after the Declaration of Independence, the date of statehood is based on when they ratified (accepted) the U.S. Constitution. Today, the United States has 50 states.

65. What happened at the Constitutional Convention?

- The Constitution was written.
- The Founding Fathers wrote the Constitution.

The Constitutional Convention was held in Philadelphia, Pennsylvania, from May to September 1787. Fifty-five delegates from 12 of the original 13 states (except for Rhode Island) met to write amendments to the Articles of Confederation. The delegates met because many American leaders did not like the Articles. The national government under the Articles of Confederation was not strong enough. Instead of changing the Articles of Confederation, the delegates decided to create a new governing document with a stronger national government—the Constitution. Each state sent delegates, who worked for four months in secret to allow for free and open discussion as they wrote the new document. The delegates who attended the Constitutional Convention are called "the Framers." On September 17, 1787, 39 of the delegates signed the new Constitution.

66. When was the Constitution written?

- 1787

The Constitution, written in 1787, created a new system of U.S. government—the same system we have today. James Madison was the main writer of the Constitution. He became the fourth president of the United States. The U.S. Constitution is short, but it defines the principles of government and the rights of citizens in the United States. The document has a preamble and seven articles. Since its adoption, the Constitution has been amended (changed) 27 times. Three-fourths of the states (9 of the original 13) were required to ratify (approve) the Constitution. Delaware was the first state to ratify the Constitution on December 7, 1787. In 1788, New Hampshire was the ninth state to ratify the Constitution. On March 4, 1789, the Constitution took effect and Congress met for the first time. George Washington was inaugurated as president the same year. By 1790, all 13 states had ratified the Constitution.

67. The Federalist Papers supported the passage of the U.S. Constitution. Name one of the writers.

- (James) Madison
- (Alexander) Hamilton
- (John) Jay
- Publius

The Federalist Papers were 85 essays that were printed in New York newspapers while New York State was deciding whether or not to support the U.S. Constitution. The essays were written in 1787 and 1788 by Alexander Hamilton, John Jay, and James Madison under the pen name "Publius." The essays explained why the state should ratify the Constitution. Other newspapers outside New York also published the essays as other states were deciding to ratify the Constitution. In 1788, the papers were published together in a book called The Federalist. Today, people still read the Federalist Papers to help them understand the Constitution.

68. What is one thing Benjamin Franklin is famous for?

- U.S. diplomat
- oldest member of the Constitutional Convention
- first Postmaster General of the United States
- writer of "Poor Richard's Almanac"
- started the first free libraries

Benjamin Franklin was one of the most influential Founding Fathers of the United States. He was the oldest delegate to the Constitutional Convention and one of the signers of the U.S. Constitution. He was a printer, author, politician, diplomat, and inventor. By his mid-20s, he was an accomplished printer, and he began writing books and papers. Franklin's most famous publication was Poor Richard's Almanac. He also organized America's first library. Its members loaned books to one another. He was very active in colonial politics. He also visited England and France many times as a U.S. diplomat. In 1775, the Second Continental Congress appointed Franklin the first postmaster general.

69. Who is the "Father of Our Country"?

- (George) Washington

George Washington is called the Father of Our Country. He was the first American president. Before that, he was a brave general who led the Continental Army to victory over Great Britain during the American Revolutionary War. After his victory over the British Army, Washington retired to his farm in Virginia named Mount Vernon. He left retirement to help create the new country's system of government. He presided over the Constitutional Convention in Philadelphia in 1787.

70. Who was the first President?*

- (George) Washington

George Washington was the first president of the United States. He began his first term in 1789. He served for a second term beginning in 1793. Washington played an important role in forming the new nation and encouraged Americans to unite. He also helped define the American presidency. He voluntarily resigned from the presidency after two terms. He set an example for future leaders in his own country and the world by voluntarily giving up power. The tradition of a president serving no more than two terms continued in the United States until Franklin D. Roosevelt, who was elected to office four times (1933–1945). The 22nd Amendment to the Constitution, passed in 1947, now limits presidents to two terms.

B: 1800s

71. What territory did the United States buy from France in 1803?

- the Louisiana Territory
- Louisiana

The Louisiana Territory was a large area west of the Mississippi River. It was 828,000 square miles. In 1803, the United States bought the Louisiana Territory from France for $15 million. The Louisiana Purchase Treaty was signed in Paris on April 30, 1803. It was the largest acquisition of land in American history. Farmers could now ship their farm products down the Mississippi River without permission from other countries. This was important because the city of New Orleans was a major shipping port. The Louisiana Purchase doubled the size of the United States and expanded it westward. Meriwether Lewis and William Clark led an expedition to map the Louisiana Territory.

72. Name one war fought by the United States in the 1800s.

- War of 1812
- Mexican-American War
- Civil War
- Spanish-American War

The United States fought four major wars in the 1800s—the War of 1812, the Mexican-American War, the Civil War, and the Spanish-American War.

The War of 1812 lasted from 1812 through 1815. President James Madison asked Congress to declare war on Great Britain. The British were stopping and seizing American ships. They were also arming American Indians to fight against the Americans. As a result of this war, the nation's trade was disrupted and the U.S. Capitol was burned. The Americans won the war. This was the first time after the Revolutionary War that America had to fight a foreign country to protect its independence.

The Mexican-American War was a conflict between Mexico and America. The war began in Texas in 1846. President James Polk ordered General Zachary Taylor and his forces to occupy land claimed by both the United States and Mexico. President Polk believed westward expansion was important for the United States to grow. When Mexico attacked, the United States went to war with Mexico. When the war ended in February 1848, the United States and Mexico signed the Treaty of Guadalupe Hidalgo. This treaty gave Texas to the United States and extended the boundaries of the United States west to the Pacific Ocean.

In the Civil War, the people of the United States fought against each other. Americans in the northern states fought to support the federal government ("the Union") against Americans from the southern states. The southern states were trying to separate themselves to form a new nation, the Confederate States of America ("the Confederacy"). The war lasted from 1861 to 1865, when the Confederate army surrendered to the Union army. Many lives were lost in the American Civil War.

In 1898, the United States fought Spain in the Spanish-American War. The United States wanted to help Cuba become independent from Spain because the United States had economic interests in Cuba. The war began when a U.S. battleship was sunk near Cuba. Many Americans believed it was the Spanish who attacked the ship. For this reason, America went to war with Spain. By the end of 1898, the war was over with a victory for the United States. Cuba had its independence, and Guam, Puerto Rico, and the Philippines became territories of the United States.

73. Name the U.S. war between the North and the South.

- the Civil War
- the War between the States

The American Civil War is also known as the War between the States. It was a war between the people in the northern states and those in the southern states. The Civil War was fought in many places across the United States, but most battles were fought in the southern states. The first battle was at Fort Sumter, South Carolina. The first major battle between the northern (Union) army and the southern (Confederate) army took place at Bull Run, in Manassas, Virginia, in July 1861. The Union expected the war to end quickly. After its defeat at the Battle of Bull Run, the Union realized that the war would be long and difficult. In 1865, the Civil War ended with the capture of the Confederate capital in Richmond, Virginia. Confederate General Robert E. Lee surrendered to Lt. General Ulysses S. Grant of the Union army at Appomattox Courthouse in central Virginia. Over the four-year period, more than 3 million Americans fought in the Civil War and more than 600,000 people died.

74. Name one problem that led to the Civil War.

- slavery
- economic reasons
- states' rights

The Civil War began when 11 southern states voted to secede (separate) from the United States to form their own country, the Confederate States of America. These southern states believed that the federal government of the United States threatened their right to make their own decisions. They wanted states' rights with each state making their own decisions about their government. If the national government contradicted the state, they did not want to follow the national government. The North and South had very different economic systems. The South's agriculture-based economy depended heavily on slave labor. The southern states feared that the United States government would end slavery. The southern states believed that this would hurt their economic and political independence. The economy of the northern states was more industrial and did not depend on slavery. The northern states fought to keep all the United States together in "the Union." They tried to stop the southern states from separating into a new Confederate nation. There were also many people in the North who wanted to end slavery. These differences led to the American Civil War, which lasted from 1861 until 1865.

75. What was one important thing that Abraham Lincoln did?*

- freed the slaves (Emancipation Proclamation)
- saved (or preserved) the Union
- led the United States during the Civil War

Abraham Lincoln was president of the United States from 1861 to 1865, and led the nation during the Civil War. Lincoln thought the separation of the southern (Confederate) states was unconstitutional, and he wanted to preserve the Union. In 1863, during the Civil War, he issued the Emancipation Proclamation. It declared that the slaves who lived in the rebelling Confederate states were forever free. Lincoln is also famous for his "Gettysburg Address." He gave that speech at Gettysburg, Pennsylvania, in November 1863. Earlier that year, at the Battle of Gettysburg, the northern (Union) army had won a major battle to stop the Confederate army from invading the North. To honor the many who died in this battle, the governor of Pennsylvania established the Soldiers' National Cemetery at Gettysburg. Lincoln spoke at the dedication ceremony and praised those who fought and died in battle. He asked those still living to rededicate themselves to saving the Union so that "government of the people, by the people, for the people shall not perish from the earth." On April 14, 1865, soon after taking office for his second term, Abraham Lincoln was killed by a southern supporter, John Wilkes Booth, at Ford's Theatre in Washington, D.C.

76. What did the Emancipation Proclamation do?

- freed the slaves
- freed slaves in the Confederacy
- freed slaves in the Confederate states
- freed slaves in most Southern states

In 1863, in the middle of the Civil War, President Abraham Lincoln issued the Emancipation Proclamation. The Emancipation Proclamation declared that slaves living in the southern or Confederate states were free. Many slaves joined the Union army. In 1865, the Civil War ended and the southern slaves kept their right to be free. The Emancipation Proclamation led to the 13th Amendment to the Constitution, which ended slavery in all of the United States.

77. What did Susan B. Anthony do?

- fought for women's rights
- fought for civil rights

Susan B. Anthony was born in Massachusetts on February 15, 1820. She is known for campaigning for the right of women to vote. She spoke out publicly against slavery and for equal treatment of women in the workplace. In 1920, the 19th Amendment to the Constitution gave women the right to vote. Susan B. Anthony died 14 years before the adoption of the 19th Amendment, but it was still widely known as the Susan B. Anthony Amendment. In 1979, she became the first woman whose image appeared on a circulating U.S. coin. The coin is called the Susan B. Anthony dollar and is worth one dollar.

C: Recent American History and Other Important Historical Information

78. Name one war fought by the United States in the 1900s.*

- World War I
- World War II
- Korean War
- Vietnam War
- (Persian) Gulf War

The United States fought five wars in the 1900s: World War I, World War II, the Korean War, the Vietnam War, and the (Persian) Gulf War.

World War I began in 1914. It was a long and bloody struggle. The United States entered the war in 1917 after German submarines attacked British and U.S. ships, and the Germans contacted Mexico about starting a war against the United States. The war ended in 1918 when the Allied Powers (led by Britain, France, Italy, and the United States) defeated the Central Powers (led by Germany, Austria-Hungary, and the Ottoman Empire). The Treaty of Versailles officially ended the war in 1919. World War I was called "the war to end all wars."

World War II began in 1939 when Germany invaded Poland. France and Great Britain then declared war on Germany. Germany had alliances with Italy and Japan, and together they formed the Axis powers. The United States entered World War II in 1941, after the Japanese attacked Pearl Harbor, Hawaii. The United States joined France, Great Britain, and the Soviet Union as the Allied powers and led the 1944 invasion of France known as D-Day. The liberation of Europe from German power was completed by May 1945. World War II did not end until Japan surrendered in September 1945.

The Korean War began in 1950 when the North Korean Army moved across the 38th parallel into South Korea. The 38th parallel was a boundary established after World War II. This boundary separated the northern area of Korea, which was under communist influence, from the southern area of Korea, which was allied with the United States. At the time, the United States was providing support to establish a democratic South Korean government. The United States provided military support to stop the advance of the North Korean Army. In the Korean conflict, democratic governments directly confronted communist governments. The fighting ended in 1953, with the establishment of the countries of North Korea and South Korea.

From 1959 to 1975, United States Armed Forces and the South Vietnamese Army fought against the North Vietnamese in the Vietnam War. The United States supported the democratic government in the south of the country to help it resist pressure from the communist north. The war ended in 1975 with the fall of Saigon, the capital of South Vietnam. In 1976, Vietnam was under total communist control. Almost 60,000 American men and women in the military died or were missing as a result of the Vietnam War.

On August 2, 1990, the Persian Gulf War began when Iraq invaded Kuwait. This invasion put the Iraqi Army closer to Saudi Arabia and its oil reserves, which supplied much of the world with oil. The United States and many other countries wanted to drive the Iraqi Army out of Kuwait and prevent it from invading other nearby countries. In January 1991, the United States led an international coalition of forces authorized by the United Nations into battle against the Iraqi Army. Within a month, the coalition had driven the Iraqis from Kuwait. The coalition declared a cease-fire on February 28, 1991.

79. Who was President during World War I?

- (Woodrow) Wilson

Woodrow Wilson was the 28th president of the United States. President Wilson served two terms from 1913 to 1921. During his first term, he was able to keep the United States out of World War I. By 1917, Wilson knew this was no longer possible, and he asked Congress to declare war on Germany. On January 8, 1918, he made a speech to Congress outlining "Fourteen Points" that justified the war and called for a plan to maintain peace after the war. President Wilson said, "We entered this war because violations of right had occurred which touched us to the quick and made the life of our own people impossible unless they were corrected and the world secure once for all against their recurrence." The war ended that year and Wilson traveled to Paris to work out the details of the surrender by Germany.

80. Who was President during the Great Depression and World War II?

- (Franklin) Roosevelt

Franklin Delano Roosevelt (FDR) was president of the United States from 1933 until 1945. He was elected during the Great Depression, which was a period of economic crisis after the stock market crash of 1929. His program for handling the crisis was called "the New Deal." It included programs to create jobs and provided benefits and financial security for workers across the country. Under his leadership, the Social Security Administration (SSA) was established in 1935. Roosevelt led the nation into World War II after Japan's attack on Pearl Harbor in December 1941. He gave the country a sense of hope and strength during a time of great struggle. Roosevelt was elected to office four times. He died in 1945, early in his fourth term as president. His wife, Eleanor Roosevelt, was a human rights leader throughout her lifetime.

81. Who did the United States fight in World War II?

- Japan, Germany, and Italy

The Japanese bombed U.S. naval bases in a surprise attack on Pearl Harbor, Hawaii, on December 7, 1941. The next day, President Franklin D. Roosevelt, as commander in chief of the military, obtained an official declaration of war from Congress. Japan's partners in the Axis, Italy and Germany, then declared war on the United States. The Allies fought against the German Nazis, the Italian Fascists, and Japan's military empire. This was truly a world war, with battles fought in Europe, Africa, Asia, and the Pacific Ocean.

82. Before he was President, Eisenhower was a general. What war was he in?

- World War II

Before becoming the 34th president of the United States in 1953, Dwight D. Eisenhower served as a major general in World War II. As commander of U.S. forces and supreme commander of the Allies in Europe, he led the successful D-Day invasion of Normandy, France, on June 6, 1944. In 1952, he retired from active service in the military. He was elected president of the United States later that year. As president, he established the interstate highway system and in 1953, the Department of Health, Education, and Welfare (now known as Health and Human Services) was created. He oversaw the end of the Korean War. Eisenhower left the White House in 1961, after serving two terms as president.

83. During the Cold War, what was the main concern of the United States?

- Communism

The main concern of the United States during the Cold War was the spread of communism. The Soviet Union (Union of Soviet Socialist Republics, or USSR) was a powerful nation that operated under the principles of communism. The United States and its allies believed that a democratic government and a capitalist economy were the best ways to preserve individual rights and freedoms. The United States and its allies feared the expansion of communism to countries outside the Soviet Union. The Cold War began shortly after the end of World War II and lasted for more than 40 years. It ended with the fall of the Berlin Wall in 1989, the reunification of East and West Germany in 1990, and the breakup of the USSR in 1991.

84. What movement tried to end racial discrimination?

- civil rights (movement)

The modern civil rights movement in the United States began in 1954 when the Supreme Court ruled that racial segregation in public schools was unconstitutional. The goal of the civil rights movement was to end racial discrimination against African Americans and to gain full and equal rights for Americans of all races. Using nonviolent strategies such as bus boycotts, sit-ins, and marches, people came together to demand social change. As a result, Congress passed the Civil Rights Act of 1964 and the Voting Rights Act of 1965. The Civil Rights Act made segregation in public facilities and racial discrimination in employment and education illegal. The law protects African Americans, women, and others from discrimination. The Voting Rights Act banned literacy tests and other special requirements that had been used to stop African Americans from registering to vote.

85. What did Martin Luther King, Jr. do?*

- fought for civil rights
- worked for equality for all Americans

Martin Luther King, Jr. was a Baptist minister and civil rights leader. He worked hard to make America a more fair, tolerant, and equal nation. He was the main leader of the civil rights movement of the 1950s and 1960s. Because of this movement, civil rights laws were passed to protect voting rights and end racial segregation. King believed in the ideals of the Declaration of Independence—that every citizen deserves America's promise of equality and justice. In 1963, King delivered his famous "I Have a Dream" speech, which imagines an America in which people of all races exist together equally. He was only 35 years old when he received the Nobel Peace Prize in 1964 for his civil rights work. King was killed on April 4, 1968.

86. What major event happened on September 11, 2001, in the United States?

- Terrorists attacked the United States.

On September 11, 2001, four airplanes flying out of U.S. airports were taken over by terrorists from the Al-Qaeda network of Islamic extremists. Two of the planes crashed into the World Trade Center's Twin Towers in New York City, destroying both buildings. One of the planes crashed into the Pentagon in Arlington, Virginia. The fourth plane, originally aimed at Washington, D.C., crashed in a field in Pennsylvania. Almost 3,000 people died in these attacks, most of them civilians. This was the worst attack on American soil in the history of the nation.

87. Name one American Indian tribe in the United States.

[USCIS Officers will be supplied with a list of federally recognized American Indian tribes.]

Cherokee	Oneida
Cheyenne	Apache
Navajo	Lakota
Arawak	Iroquois
Sioux	Crow
Shawnee	Creek
Chippewa	Teton
Mohegan	Blackfeet
Choctaw	Hopi
Huron	Seminole
Pueblo	Inuit

American Indians lived in North America for thousands of years before the European settlers arrived. Today there are more than 500 federally recognized tribes in the United States. Each tribe has its own social and political system. American Indian cultures are different from one tribe to another, with different languages, beliefs, stories, music, and foods. Earlier in their history, some tribes settled in villages and farmed the land for food.

Other tribes moved frequently as they hunted and gathered food and resources. The federal government signed treaties with American Indian tribes to move the tribes to reservations. These reservations are recognized as domestic, dependent nations.

Integrated Civics

An understanding of America's geography, symbols, and holidays is important. They provide background and more meaning to historical events and other landmark moments in U.S. history. The following section offers short lessons on our country's geography, national symbols, and national holidays. The geography of the United States is unusual because of the size of the country and the fact that it is bordered by two oceans that create natural boundaries to the east and west. Through visual symbols such as our flag and the Statue of Liberty, the values and history of the United States are often expressed. Finally, you will also learn about our national holidays and why we celebrate them. Most of our holidays honor people who have contributed to our history and to the development of our nation. By learning this information, you will develop a deeper understanding of the United States and its geographical boundaries, principles, and freedoms.

A: Geography

88. Name one of the two longest rivers in the United States.

- Missouri (River)
- Mississippi (River)

The Mississippi River is one of America's longest rivers. It runs through 10 U.S. states. The Mississippi River was used by American Indians for trade, food, and water before Europeans came to America. It is nicknamed the "Father of Waters." Today, the Mississippi River is a major shipping route and a source of drinking water for millions of people. The Missouri River is also one of the longest rivers in the United States. The Missouri River is actually longer than the Mississippi River. It starts in Montana and flows into the Mississippi River. In 1673, the French explorers Jolliet and Marquette were the first Europeans to find the Missouri River. It is nicknamed "Big Muddy" because of its high silt content.

89. What ocean is on the West Coast of the United States?

- Pacific (Ocean)

The Pacific Ocean is on the West Coast of the United States. It is the largest ocean on Earth and covers one-third of the Earth's surface. The Pacific Ocean is important to the U.S. economy because of its many natural resources such as fish. Europeans first learned about the Pacific Ocean in the 16th century. Spanish explorer Vasco Núñez de Balboa reached the ocean in 1514 when he crossed the Isthmus of Panama. Later, Ferdinand Magellan sailed across the Pacific as he traveled around the Earth in search of spices. "Pacific" means "peaceful." Magellan named the Pacific Ocean the "peaceful sea," because there were no storms on his trip from Spain to the spice world. The U.S. states that border the Pacific Ocean are Alaska, Washington, Oregon, California, and Hawaii.

90. What ocean is on the East Coast of the United States?

- Atlantic (Ocean)

The Atlantic Ocean is on the East Coast of the United States. The ocean was named after the giant Atlas from Greek mythology. It is the second largest ocean in the world. The Atlantic Ocean is a major sea route for ships. It is one of the most frequently traveled oceans in the world. The Atlantic Ocean is also a source of many natural resources. The Atlantic Ocean was formed by the separation of the North American and European continents millions of years ago. The ocean covers about one-fifth of the Earth's surface. In the middle of the ocean is the Mid-Atlantic Ridge, an immense underwater mountain range that extends the length of the Atlantic and is a source of volcanic activity. The U.S. states that border the Atlantic Ocean are Connecticut, Delaware, Florida, Georgia, Maine, Maryland, Massachusetts, New Hampshire, New Jersey, New York, North Carolina, Rhode Island, South Carolina, and Virginia.

91. Name one U.S. territory.

- Puerto Rico
- U.S. Virgin Islands
- American Samoa
- Northern Mariana Islands
- Guam

There are five major U.S. territories: American Samoa, Guam, the Northern Mariana Islands, Puerto Rico, and the U.S. Virgin Islands. A U.S. territory is a partially self-governing piece of land under the authority of the U.S. government. U.S. territories are not states, but they do have representation in Congress. Each territory is allowed to send a delegate to the House of Representatives. The people who live in American Samoa are considered U.S. nationals; the people in the other four territories are U.S. citizens. Citizens of the territories can vote in primary elections for president, but they cannot vote in the general elections for president.

92. Name one state that borders Canada.

Maine	Idaho
Minnesota	Pennsylvania
New Hampshire	Washington
North Dakota	Ohio
Vermont	Alaska
Montana	Michigan
New York	

The northern border of the United States stretches more than 5,000 miles from Maine in the East to Alaska in the West. There are 13 states on the border with Canada. The Treaty of Paris of 1783 established the official boundary between Canada and the United States after the Revolutionary War. Since that time, there have been land disputes, but they have been resolved through treaties. The International Boundary Commission, which is headed by two commissioners, one American and one Canadian, is responsible for maintaining the boundary.

93. Name one state that borders Mexico.

- California
- Arizona
- New Mexico
- Texas

The border between the United States and Mexico is about 1,900 miles long and spans four U.S. states— Arizona, California, New Mexico, and Texas. The United States established the border with Mexico after the Mexican-American War and the Gadsden Purchase in 1853. The Gadsden Purchase helped the United States get the land it needed to expand the southern railroad. The United States bought this land for $10 million. The land bought through the Gadsden Purchase is now part of the states of Arizona and New Mexico. The U.S. border with Mexico is one of the busiest international borders in the world.

94. What is the capital of the United States?*

- Washington, D.C.

When the Constitution established our nation in 1789, the capital of the United States was in New York City. Congress soon began discussing the location of a permanent capital city. In Congress, representatives of northern states argued with representatives of southern states. Each side wanted the capital to be in its own region. As part of the Compromise of 1790, the capital would be located in the South. In return, the North did not have to pay the debt it owed from the Revolutionary War. George Washington chose a location for the capital along the Potomac River between Maryland and Virginia. As part of the compromise, Philadelphia, Pennsylvania, became the temporary new location for the capital. In 1800, after 10 years, the capital was moved to its current location of Washington, D.C.

95. Where is the Statue of Liberty?*

- New York (Harbor)
- Liberty Island

[Also acceptable are New Jersey, near New York City, and on the Hudson (River).]

The Statue of Liberty is on Liberty Island, a 12-acre island in the New York harbor. France gave the statue to the United States as a gift of friendship. French artist Frederic-Auguste Bartholdi made the statue. It shows a woman escaping the chains of tyranny and holding a torch symbolizing liberty. The Statue of Liberty was dedicated on October 28, 1886, 110 years after the signing of the Declaration of Independence. President Grover Cleveland accepted the gift for the American people. The Statue of Liberty is a well-known symbol of the United States and of freedom and democracy. The Statue of Liberty became a symbol of immigration because it was located next to Ellis Island, which was the first entry point for many immigrants during the great waves of immigration. The Statue of Liberty was the first thing new immigrants saw as they approached New York harbor.

B: Symbols

96. Why does the flag have 13 stripes?

- because there were 13 original colonies
- because the stripes represent the original colonies

There are 13 stripes on the flag because there were 13 original colonies. We call the American flag "the Stars and Stripes." For 18 years after the United States became an independent country, the flag had only 13 stripes. In 1794, Kentucky and Vermont joined the United States, and two stripes were added to the flag. In 1818, Congress decided that the number of stripes on the flag should always be 13. This would honor the original states that were colonies of Great Britain before America's independence.

97. Why does the flag have 50 stars?*

- because there is one star for each state
- because each star represents a state
- because there are 50 states

Each star on the flag represents a state. This is why the number of stars has changed over the years from 13 to 50. The number of stars reached 50 in 1959, when Hawaii joined the United States as the 50th state. In 1777, the Second Continental Congress passed the first Flag Act, stating, "Resolved, That the flag of the United States be made of thirteen stripes, alternate red and white; that the union be thirteen stars, white in a blue field, representing a new Constellation."

98. What is the name of the national anthem?

- The Star-Spangled Banner

During the War of 1812, British soldiers invaded the United States. On the night of September 13, 1814, British warships bombed Fort McHenry. This fort protected the city of Baltimore, Maryland. An American named Francis Scott Key watched the bombing and thought that the fort would fall. As the sun rose the next morning, Key looked toward the fort. He saw that the flag above the fort was still flying. This let him know that the British had not defeated the Americans. Key immediately wrote the words to a poem he called the "Defence of Fort M'Henry." The words of the poem became "The Star-Spangled Banner."

Congress passed a law in 1931 naming "The Star-Spangled Banner" the official national anthem. Here are the words to the first verse of the national anthem:

The Star-Spangled Banner
Oh, say, can you see, by the dawn's early light,
What so proudly we hailed at the twilight's last gleaming?
Whose broad stripes and bright stars, thro' the perilous fight;
O'er the ramparts we watched, were so gallantly streaming.
And the rockets' red glare, the bombs bursting in air,
Gave proof through the night that our flag was still there.
Oh, say, does that star-spangled banner yet wave
O'er the land of the free and the home of the brave?

C: Holidays

99. When do we celebrate Independence Day?*

- July 4

In the United States, we celebrate Independence Day on July 4 to mark the anniversary of the adoption of the Declaration of Independence. After signing the Declaration of Independence, John Adams wrote to his wife, "I am apt to believe that it will be celebrated, by succeeding Generations, as the great anniversary Festival." The Declaration of Independence, written by Thomas Jefferson, explained why the colonies had decided to separate from Great Britain. Americans celebrate the Fourth of July as the birthday of America, with parades, fireworks, patriotic songs, and readings of the Declaration of Independence.

100. Name two national U.S. holidays.

New Year's Day
Martin Luther King, Jr. Day
Presidents' Day
Memorial Day
Juneteenth
Independence Day
Labor Day
Columbus Day
Veterans Day
Thanksgiving
Christmas

Many Americans celebrate national or federal holidays. These holidays often honor people or events in our American heritage. These holidays are "national" in a legal sense only for federal institutions and in the District of Columbia. Typically, federal offices are closed on these holidays. Each state can decide whether or not to celebrate the holiday. Businesses, schools, and commercial establishments may choose whether or not to close on these days. Since 1971, federal holidays are observed on Mondays except for New Year's Day, Independence Day, Veterans Day, Thanksgiving, and Christmas.

Civics Question Pool (2008 Version)

All of the questions that you may be asked on the civics section of the citizenship interview appear here without the answers. We recommend that you practice by having someone ask you questions from this list. This is the best way to simulate what you will experience at the interview. If you prefer to practice alone or quietly, you may write your answer in the space provided.

1. What is the supreme law of the land?

2. What does the Constitution do?

3. The idea of self-government is in the first three words of the Constitution. What are these words?

4. What is an amendment?

5. What do we call the first ten amendments to the Constitution?

6. What is one right or freedom from the First Amendment?

7. How many amendments does the Constitution have?

8. What did the Declaration of Independence do?

9. What are two rights in the Declaration of Independence?

10. What is freedom of religion?

11. What is the economic system in the United States?*

12. What is the "rule of law"?

13. Name one branch or part of the government.*

14. What stops one branch of government from becoming too powerful?

15. Who is in charge of the executive branch?

16. Who makes federal laws?

17. What are the two parts of the U.S. Congress?*

18. How many U.S. Senators are there?

19. We elect a U.S. Senator for how many years?

20. Who is one of your state's U.S. Senators now?*

21. The House of Representatives has how many voting members?

22. We elect a U.S. Representative for how many years?

23. Name your U.S. Representative.

24. Who does a U.S. Senator represent?

25. Why do some states have more Representatives than other states?

26. We elect a President for how many years?

27. In what month do we vote for President?*

28. What is the name of the President of the United States now?*

29. What is the name of the Vice President of the United States now?

30. If the President can no longer serve, who becomes President?

31. If both the President and the Vice President can no longer serve, who becomes President?

32. Who is the Commander in Chief of the military?

33. Who signs bills to become laws?

34. Who vetoes bills?

35. What does the President's Cabinet do?

36. What are two Cabinet-level positions?

37. What does the judicial branch do?

38. What is the highest court in the United States?

39. How many justices are on the Supreme Court?

40. Who is the Chief Justice of the United States now?

41. Under our Constitution, some powers belong to the federal government. What is one power of the federal government?

42. Under our Constitution, some powers belong to the states. What is one power of the states?

43. Who is the Governor of your state now?

44. What is the capital of your state?*

45. What are the two major political parties in the United States?*

46. What is the political party of the President now?

47. What is the name of the Speaker of the House of Representatives now?

48. There are four amendments to the Constitution about who can vote. Describe one of them.

49. What is one responsibility that is only for United States citizens?*

50. Name one right only for United States citizens.

51. What are two rights of everyone living in the United States?

52. What do we show loyalty to when we say the Pledge of Allegiance?

53. What is one promise you make when you become a United States citizen?

54. How old do citizens have to be to vote for President?*

55. What are two ways that Americans can participate in their democracy?

56. When is the last day you can send in federal income tax forms?*

57. When must all men register for the Selective Service?

58. What is one reason colonists came to America?

59. Who lived in America before the Europeans arrived?

60. What group of people was taken to America and sold as slaves?

61. Why did the colonists fight the British?

62. Who wrote the Declaration of Independence?

63. When was the Declaration of Independence adopted?

64. There were 13 original states. Name three.

65. What happened at the Constitutional Convention?

66. When was the Constitution written?

67. The Federalist Papers supported the passage of the U.S. Constitution. Name one of the writers.

68. What is one thing Benjamin Franklin is famous for?

69. Who is the "Father of Our Country"?

70. Who was the first President?*

71. What territory did the United States buy from France in 1803?

72. Name one war fought by the United States in the 1800s.

73. Name the U.S. war between the North and the South.

74. Name one problem that led to the Civil War.

75. What was one important thing that Abraham Lincoln did?*

76. What did the Emancipation Proclamation do?

77. What did Susan B. Anthony do?

78. Name one war fought by the United States in the 1900s.*

79. Who was President during World War I?

80. Who was President during the Great Depression and World War II?

81. Who did the United States fight in World War II?

82. Before he was President, Eisenhower was a general. What war was he in?

83. During the Cold War, what was the main concern of the United States?

84. What movement tried to end racial discrimination?

85. What did Martin Luther King, Jr. do?*

86. What major event happened on September 11, 2001, in the United States?

87. Name one American Indian tribe in the United States.

88. Name one of the two longest rivers in the United States.

89. What ocean is on the West Coast of the United States?

90. What ocean is on the East Coast of the United States?

91. Name one U.S. territory.

92. Name one state that borders Canada.

93. Name one state that borders Mexico.

94. What is the capital of the United States?*

95. Where is the Statue of Liberty?*

96. Why does the flag have 13 stripes?

97. Why does the flag have 50 stars?*

98. What is the name of the national anthem?

99. When do we celebrate Independence Day?*

100. Name two national U.S. holidays.

Civics Questions and Answers (2020 Version)

Please note that this is the question pool only for applicants who filed on or after December 1, 2020 AND who are taking the test prior to April 19, 2021.

American Government

A: Principles of American Government

1. What is the form of government of the United States?

- Republic
- Constitution-based federal republic
- Representative democracy

2. What is the supreme law of the land?*

- (U.S.) Constitution

3. Name one thing the U.S. Constitution does.

- Forms the government
- Defines powers of government
- Defines the parts of government
- Protects the rights of the people

4. The U.S. Constitution starts with the words "We the People." What does "We the People" mean?

- Self-government
- Popular sovereignty
- Consent of the governed
- People should govern themselves
- (Example of) social contract

5. How are changes made to the U.S. Constitution?

- Amendments
- The amendment process

6. What does the Bill of Rights protect?

- (The basic) rights of Americans
- (The basic) rights of people living in the United States

7. How many amendments does the U.S. Constitution have?*

- Twenty-seven (27)

8. Why is the Declaration of Independence important?

- It says America is free from British control.
- It says all people are created equal.
- It identifies inherent rights.
- It identifies individual freedoms.

9. What founding document said the American colonies were free from Britain?

- Declaration of Independence

10. Name two important ideas from the Declaration of Independence and the U.S. Constitution.

- Equality
- Liberty
- Social contract
- Natural rights
- Limited government
- Self-government

11. The words "Life, Liberty, and the pursuit of Happiness" are in what founding document?

- Declaration of Independence

12. What is the economic system of the United States?*

- Capitalism
- Free market economy

13. What is the rule of law?

- Everyone must follow the law.
- Leaders must obey the law.
- Government must obey the law.
- No one is above the law.

14. Many documents influenced the U.S. Constitution. Name one.

- Declaration of Independence
- Articles of Confederation
- Federalist Papers
- Anti-Federalist Papers
- Virginia Declaration of Rights
- Fundamental Orders of Connecticut

- Mayflower Compact
- Iroquois Great Law of Peace

15. There are three branches of government. Why?

- So one part does not become too powerful
- Checks and balances
- Separation of powers

B: System of Government

16. Name the three branches of government.

- Legislative, executive, and judicial
- Congress, president, and the courts

17. The President of the United States is in charge of which branch of government?

- Executive branch

18. What part of the federal government writes laws?

- (U.S.) Congress
- (U.S. or national) legislature
- Legislative branch

19. What are the two parts of the U.S. Congress?

- Senate and House (of Representatives)

20. Name one power of the U.S. Congress.*

- Writes laws
- Declares war
- Makes the federal budget

21. How many U.S. senators are there?

- One hundred (100)

22. How long is a term for a U.S. senator?

- Six (6) years

23. Who is one of your state's U.S. senators now?

- Answers will vary. [District of Columbia residents and residents of U.S. territories should answer that D.C. (or the territory where the applicant lives) has no U.S. Senators.]

For a complete list of U.S. senators and the states they represent, go to www.senate.gov.

24. How many voting members are in the House of Representatives?

- Four hundred thirty-five (435)

25. How long is a term for a member of the House of Representatives?

- Two (2) years

26. Why do U.S. representatives serve shorter terms than U.S. senators?

- To more closely follow public opinion

27. How many senators does each state have?

- Two (2)

28. Why does each state have two senators?

- Equal representation (for small states)
- The Great Compromise (Connecticut Compromise)

29. Name your U.S. representative.

- Answers will vary. [Residents of territories with nonvoting Delegates or Resident Commissioners may provide the name of that Delegate or Commissioner. Also acceptable is any statement that the territory has no (voting) Representatives in Congress.]

For a complete list of U.S. representatives and the districts they represent, go to: www.house.gov.

30. What is the name of the Speaker of the House of Representatives now?*

- Visit https://www.uscis.gov/citizenship/testupdates for the name of the Speaker of the House of Representatives.

31. Who does a U.S. senator represent?

- Citizens of their state

32. Who elects U.S. senators?

- Citizens from their state

33. Who does a member of the House of Representatives represent?

- Citizens in their (congressional) district
- Citizens in their district

34. Who elects members of the House of Representatives?

- Citizens from their (congressional) district

35. Some states have more representatives than other states. Why?

- (Because of) the state's population
- (Because) they have more people
- (Because) some states have more people

36. The President of the United States is elected for how many years?*

- Four (4) years

37. The President of the United States can serve only two terms. Why?

- (Because of) the 22nd Amendment
- To keep the president from becoming too powerful

38. What is the name of the President of the United States now?*

- Visit https://www.uscis.gov/citizenship/testupdates for the name of the President of the United States.

39. What is the name of the Vice President of the United States now?*

- Visit https://www.uscis.gov/citizenship/testupdates for the name of the Vice President of the United States.

40. If the president can no longer serve, who becomes president?

- The Vice President (of the United States)

41. Name one power of the president.

- Signs bills into law
- Vetoes bills
- Enforces laws
- Commander in Chief (of the military)
- Chief diplomat

42. Who is Commander in Chief of the U.S. military?

- The President (of the United States)

43. Who signs bills to become laws?

- The President (of the United States)

44. Who vetoes bills?*

- The President (of the United States)

45. Who appoints federal judges?

- The President (of the United States)

46. The executive branch has many parts. Name one.

- President (of the United States)
- Cabinet
- Federal departments and agencies

47. What does the President's Cabinet do?

- Advises the President (of the United States)

48. What are two Cabinet-level positions?

- Attorney General
- Secretary of Agriculture
- Secretary of Commerce
- Secretary of Defense
- Secretary of Education
- Secretary of Energy
- Secretary of Health and Human Services
- Secretary of Homeland Security
- Secretary of Housing and Urban Development
- Secretary of the Interior
- Secretary of Labor
- Secretary of State
- Secretary of Transportation
- Secretary of the Treasury
- Secretary of Veterans Affairs
- Vice President (of the United States)

49. Why is the Electoral College important?

- It decides who is elected president.
- It provides a compromise between the popular election of the president and congressional selection.

50. What is one part of the judicial branch?

- Supreme Court
- Federal Courts

51. What does the judicial branch do?

- Reviews laws
- Explains laws
- Resolves disputes (disagreements) about the law
- Decides if a law goes against the (U.S.) Constitution

52. What is the highest court in the United States?*

- Supreme Court

53. How many seats are on the Supreme Court?

- Nine (9)

54. How many Supreme Court justices are usually needed to decide a case?

- Five (5)

55. How long do Supreme Court justices serve?

- (For) life
- Lifetime appointment
- (Until) retirement

56. Supreme Court justices serve for life. Why?

- To be independent (of politics)
- To limit outside (political) influence

57. Who is the Chief Justice of the United States now?

- Visit https://www.uscis.gov/citizenship/testupdates for the name of the Chief Justice of the United States.

58. Name one power that is only for the federal government.

- Print paper money
- Mint coins
- Declare war
- Create an army
- Make treaties
- Set foreign policy

59. Name one power that is only for the states.

- Provide schooling and education
- Provide protection (police)

- Provide safety (fire departments)
- Give a driver's license
- Approve zoning and land use

60. What is the purpose of the 10th Amendment?

- (It states that the) powers not given to the federal government belong to the states or to the people.

61. Who is the governor of your state now?*

- Answers will vary. [District of Columbia residents should answer that D.C. does not have a governor.]

62. What is the capital of your state?

- Answers will vary. [District of Columbia residents should answer that D.C. is not a state and does not have a capital. Residents of U.S. territories should name the capital of the territory.]

C: Rights and Responsibilities

63. There are four amendments to the U.S. Constitution about who can vote. Describe one of them.

- Citizens eighteen (18) and older (can vote).
- You don't have to pay (a poll tax) to vote.
- Any citizen can vote. (Women and men can vote.)
- A male citizen of any race (can vote).

64. Who can vote in federal elections, run for federal office, and serve on a jury in the United States?

- Citizens
- Citizens of the United States
- U.S. citizens

65. What are three rights of everyone living in the United States?

- Freedom of expression
- Freedom of speech
- Freedom of assembly
- Freedom to petition the government
- Freedom of religion
- The right to bear arms

66. What do we show loyalty to when we say the Pledge of Allegiance?*

- The United States
- The flag

67. Name two promises that new citizens make in the Oath of Allegiance.

- Give up loyalty to other countries
- Defend the (U.S.) Constitution
- Obey the laws of the United States
- Serve in the military (if needed)
- Serve (help, do important work for) the nation (if needed)
- Be loyal to the United States

68. How can people become United States citizens?

- Naturalize
- Derive citizenship
- Be born in the United States

69. What are two examples of civic participation in the United States?

- Vote
- Run for office
- Join a political party
- Help with a campaign
- Join a civic group
- Join a community group
- Give an elected official your opinion (on an issue)
- Contact elected officials
- Support or oppose an issue or policy
- Write to a newspaper

70. What is one way Americans can serve their country?

- Vote
- Pay taxes
- Obey the law
- Serve in the military
- Run for office
- Work for local, state, or federal government

71. Why is it important to pay federal taxes?

- Required by law
- All people pay to fund the federal government

- Required by the (U.S.) Constitution (16th Amendment)
- Civic duty

72. It is important for all men age 18 through 25 to register for the Selective Service. Name one reason why.

- Required by law
- Civic duty
- Makes the draft fair, if needed

American History

A: Colonial Period and Independence

73. The colonists came to America for many reasons. Name one.

- Freedom
- Political liberty
- Religious freedom
- Economic opportunity
- Escape persecution

74. Who lived in America before the Europeans arrived?*

- American Indians
- Native Americans

75. What group of people was taken and sold as slaves?

- Africans
- People from Africa

76. What war did the Americans fight to win independence from Britain?

- American Revolution
- The (American) Revolutionary War
- War for (American) Independence

77. Name one reason why the Americans declared independence from Britain.

- High taxes
- Taxation without representation
- British soldiers stayed in Americans' houses (boarding, quartering)
- They did not have self-government
- Boston Massacre
- Boston Tea Party (Tea Act)
- Stamp Act
- Sugar Act

- Townshend Acts
- Intolerable (Coercive) Acts

78. Who wrote the Declaration of Independence?*

- (Thomas) Jefferson

79. When was the Declaration of Independence adopted?

- July 4, 1776

80. The American Revolution had many important events. Name one.

- (Battle of) Bunker Hill
- Declaration of Independence
- Washington Crossing the Delaware (Battle of Trenton)
- (Battle of) Saratoga
- Valley Forge (Encampment)
- (Battle of) Yorktown (British surrender at Yorktown)

81. There were 13 original states. Name five.

- New Hampshire
- Massachusetts
- Rhode Island
- Connecticut
- New York
- New Jersey
- Pennsylvania
- Delaware
- Maryland
- Virginia
- North Carolina
- South Carolina
- Georgia

82. What founding document was written in 1787?

- (U.S.) Constitution

83. The Federalist Papers supported the passage of the U.S. Constitution. Name one of the writers.

- (James) Madison
- (Alexander) Hamilton
- (John) Jay
- Publius

84. Why were the Federalist Papers important?

- They helped people understand the (U.S.) Constitution.
- They supported passing the (U.S.) Constitution.

85. Benjamin Franklin is famous for many things. Name one.

- Founded the first free public libraries
- First Postmaster General of the United States
- Helped write the Declaration of Independence
- Inventor
- U.S. diplomat

86. George Washington is famous for many things. Name one.*

- "Father of Our Country"
- First president of the United States
- General of the Continental Army
- President of the Constitutional Convention

87. Thomas Jefferson is famous for many things. Name one.

- Writer of the Declaration of Independence
- Third president of the United States
- Doubled the size of the United States (Louisiana Purchase)
- First Secretary of State
- Founded the University of Virginia
- Writer of the Virginia Statute on Religious Freedom

88. James Madison is famous for many things. Name one.

- "Father of the Constitution"
- Fourth president of the United States
- President during the War of 1812
- One of the writers of the Federalist Papers

89. Alexander Hamilton is famous for many things. Name one.

- First Secretary of the Treasury
- One of the writers of the Federalist Papers
- Helped establish the First Bank of the United States
- Aide to General George Washington
- Member of the Continental Congress

B: 1800s

90. What territory did the United States buy from France in 1803?

- Louisiana Territory
- Louisiana

91. Name one war fought by the United States in the 1800s.

- War of 1812
- Mexican-American War
- Civil War
- Spanish-American War

92. Name the U.S. war between the North and the South.

- The Civil War

93. The Civil War had many important events. Name one.

- (Battle of) Fort Sumter
- Emancipation Proclamation
- (Battle of) Vicksburg
- (Battle of) Gettysburg
- Sherman's March
- (Surrender at) Appomattox
- (Battle of) Antietam/Sharpsburg
- Lincoln was assassinated.

94. Abraham Lincoln is famous for many things. Name one.*

- Freed the slaves (Emancipation Proclamation)
- Saved (or preserved) the Union
- Led the United States during the Civil War
- 16th president of the United States
- Delivered the Gettysburg Address

95. What did the Emancipation Proclamation do?

- Freed the slaves
- Freed slaves in the Confederacy
- Freed slaves in the Confederate states
- Freed slaves in most Southern states

96. What U.S. war ended slavery?

- The Civil War

97. What amendment gives citizenship to all persons born in the United States?

- 14th Amendment

98. When did all men get the right to vote?

- After the Civil War
- During Reconstruction
- (With the) 15th Amendment
- 1870

99. Name one leader of the women's rights movement in the 1800s.

- Susan B. Anthony
- Elizabeth Cady Stanton
- Sojourner Truth
- Harriet Tubman
- Lucretia Mott
- Lucy Stone

C: Recent American History and Other Important Historical Information

100. Name one war fought by the United States in the 1900s.

- World War I
- World War II
- Korean War
- Vietnam War
- (Persian) Gulf War

101. Why did the United States enter World War I?

- Because Germany attacked U.S. (civilian) ships
- To support the Allied Powers (England, France, Italy, and Russia)
- To oppose the Central Powers (Germany, Austria-Hungary, the Ottoman Empire, and Bulgaria)

102. When did all women get the right to vote?

- 1920
- After World War I
- (With the) 19th Amendment

103. What was the Great Depression?

- Longest economic recession in modern history

104. When did the Great Depression start?

- The Great Crash (1929)
- Stock market crash of 1929

105. Who was president during the Great Depression and World War II?

- (Franklin) Roosevelt

106. Why did the United States enter World War II?

- (Bombing of) Pearl Harbor
- Japanese attacked Pearl Harbor
- To support the Allied Powers (England, France, and Russia)
- To oppose the Axis Powers (Germany, Italy, and Japan)

107. Dwight Eisenhower is famous for many things. Name one.

- General during World War II
- President at the end of (during) the Korean War
- 34th president of the United States
- Signed the Federal-Aid Highway Act of 1956 (Created the Interstate System)

108. Who was the United States' main rival during the Cold War?

- Soviet Union
- USSR
- Russia

109. During the Cold War, what was one main concern of the United States?

- Communism
- Nuclear war

110. Why did the United States enter the Korean War?

- To stop the spread of communism

111. Why did the United States enter the Vietnam War?

- To stop the spread of communism

112. What did the civil rights movement do?

- Fought to end racial discrimination

113. Martin Luther King, Jr. is famous for many things. Name one.*

- Fought for civil rights
- Worked for equality for all Americans
- Worked to ensure that people would "not be judged by the color of their skin, but by the content of their character"

114. Why did the United States enter the Persian Gulf War?

- To force the Iraqi military from Kuwait

115. What major event happened on September 11, 2001 in the United States?*

- Terrorists attacked the United States
- Terrorists took over two planes and crashed them into the World Trade Center in New York City
- Terrorists took over a plane and crashed into the Pentagon in Arlington, Virginia
- Terrorists took over a plane originally aimed at Washington, D.C., and crashed in a field in Pennsylvania

116. Name one U.S. military conflict after the September 11, 2001 attacks.

- (Global) War on Terror
- War in Afghanistan
- War in Iraq

117. Name one American Indian tribe in the United States.

- Apache
- Blackfeet
- Cayuga
- Cherokee
- Cheyenne
- Chippewa
- Choctaw
- Creek
- Crow
- Hopi
- Huron
- Inupiat
- Lakota
- Mohawk
- Mohegan
- Navajo
- Oneida
- Onondaga
- Pueblo

- Seminole
- Seneca
- Shawnee
- Sioux
- Teton
- Tuscarora
- For a complete list of tribes, please visit https://www.bia.gov/.

118. Name one example of an American innovation.

- Light bulb
- Automobile (cars, internal combustion engine)
- Skyscrapers
- Airplane
- Assembly line
- Landing on the moon
- Integrated circuit (IC)

Symbols and Holidays

A: Symbols

119. What is the capital of the United States?

- Washington, D.C.

120. Where is the Statue of Liberty?

- New York (Harbor)
- Liberty Island [Also acceptable are New Jersey, near New York City, and on the Hudson (River).]

121. Why does the flag have 13 stripes?*

- (Because there were) 13 original colonies
- (Because the stripes) represent the original colonies

122. Why does the flag have 50 stars?

- (Because there is) one star for each state
- (Because) each star represents a state
- (Because there are) 50 states

123. What is the name of the national anthem?

- The Star-Spangled Banner

124. The Nation's first motto was "E Pluribus Unum." What does that mean?

- Out of many, one
- We all become one

B: Holidays

125. What is Independence Day?

- A holiday to celebrate U.S. independence (from Britain)
- The country's birthday

126. Name three national U.S. holidays.*

- New Year's Day
- Martin Luther King, Jr. Day
- Presidents Day (Washington's Birthday)
- Memorial Day
- Juneteenth
- Independence Day
- Labor Day
- Columbus Day
- Veterans Day
- Thanksgiving Day
- Christmas Day

127. What is Memorial Day?

- A holiday to honor soldiers who died in military service

128. What is Veterans Day?

- A holiday to honor people in the (U.S.) military
- A holiday to honor people who have served (in the U.S. military)

Civics Question Pool (2020 Version)

All of the questions that you may be asked on the civics section of the citizenship interview appear here without the answers. We recommend that you practice by having someone ask you questions from this list. This is the best way to simulate what you will experience at the interview. If you prefer to practice alone or quietly, you may write your answer in the space provided.

Please note that this is the question pool only for applicants who filed on or after December 1, 2020 AND who are taking the test prior to April 19, 2021.

1. What is the form of government of the United States?

2. What is the supreme law of the land?*

3. Name one thing the U.S. Constitution does.

4. The U.S. Constitution starts with the words "We the People." What does "We the People" mean?

5. How are changes made to the U.S. Constitution?

6. What does the Bill of Rights protect?

7. How many amendments does the U.S. Constitution have?*

8. Why is the Declaration of Independence important?

9. What founding document said the American colonies were free from Britain?

10. Name two important ideas from the Declaration of Independence and the U.S. Constitution.

11. The words "Life, Liberty, and the pursuit of Happiness" are in what founding document?

12. What is the economic system of the United States?*

13. What is the rule of law?

14. Many documents influenced the U.S. Constitution. Name one.

15. There are three branches of government. Why?

16. Name the three branches of government.

17. The President of the United States is in charge of which branch of government?

18. What part of the federal government writes laws?

19. What are the two parts of the U.S. Congress?

20. Name one power of the U.S. Congress.*

21. How many U.S. senators are there?

22. How long is a term for a U.S. senator?

23. Who is one of your state's U.S. senators now?

24. How many voting members are in the House of Representatives?

25. How long is a term for a member of the House of Representatives?

26. Why do U.S. representatives serve shorter terms than U.S. senators?

27. How many senators does each state have?

28. Why does each state have two senators?

29. Name your U.S. representative.

30. What is the name of the Speaker of the House of Representatives now?*

31. Who does a U.S. senator represent?

32. Who elects U.S. senators?

33. Who does a member of the House of Representatives represent?

34. Who elects members of the House of Representatives?

35. Some states have more representatives than other states. Why?

36. The President of the United States is elected for how many years?*

37. The President of the United States can serve only two terms. Why?

38. What is the name of the President of the United States now?*

39. What is the name of the Vice President of the United States now?*

40. If the president can no longer serve, who becomes president?

41. Name one power of the president.

42. Who is Commander in Chief of the U.S. military?

43. Who signs bills to become laws?

44. Who vetoes bills?*

45. Who appoints federal judges?

46. The executive branch has many parts. Name one.

47. What does the President's Cabinet do?

48. What are two Cabinet-level positions?

49. Why is the Electoral College important?

50. What is one part of the judicial branch?

51. What does the judicial branch do?

52. What is the highest court in the United States?*

53. How many seats are on the Supreme Court?

54. How many Supreme Court justices are usually needed to decide a case?

55. How long do Supreme Court justices serve?

56. Supreme Court justices serve for life. Why?

57. Who is the Chief Justice of the United States now?

58. Name one power that is only for the federal government.

59. Name one power that is only for the states.

60. What is the purpose of the 10th Amendment?

61. Who is the governor of your state now?*

62. What is the capital of your state?

63. There are four amendments to the U.S. Constitution about who can vote. Describe one of them.

64. Who can vote in federal elections, run for federal office, and serve on a jury in the United States?

65. What are three rights of everyone living in the United States?

66. What do we show loyalty to when we say the Pledge of Allegiance?*

67. Name two promises that new citizens make in the Oath of Allegiance.

68. How can people become United States citizens?

69. What are two examples of civic participation in the United States?

70. What is one way Americans can serve their country?

71. Why is it important to pay federal taxes?

72. It is important for all men age 18 through 25 to register for the Selective Service. Name one reason why.

73. The colonists came to America for many reasons. Name one.

74. Who lived in America before the Europeans arrived?*

75. What group of people was taken and sold as slaves?

76. What war did the Americans fight to win independence from Britain?

77. Name one reason why the Americans declared independence from Britain.

78. Who wrote the Declaration of Independence?*

79. When was the Declaration of Independence adopted?

80. The American Revolution had many important events. Name one.

81. There were 13 original states. Name five.

82. What founding document was written in 1787?

83. The Federalist Papers supported the passage of the U.S. Constitution. Name one of the writers.

84. Why were the Federalist Papers important?

85. Benjamin Franklin is famous for many things. Name one.

86. George Washington is famous for many things. Name one.*

87. Thomas Jefferson is famous for many things. Name one.

88. James Madison is famous for many things. Name one.

89. Alexander Hamilton is famous for many things. Name one.

90. What territory did the United States buy from France in 1803?

91. Name one war fought by the United States in the 1800s.

92. Name the U.S. war between the North and the South.

93. The Civil War had many important events. Name one.

94. Abraham Lincoln is famous for many things. Name one.*

95. What did the Emancipation Proclamation do?

96. What U.S. war ended slavery?

97. What amendment gives citizenship to all persons born in the United States?

98. When did all men get the right to vote?

99. Name one leader of the women's rights movement in the 1800s.

100. Name one war fought by the United States in the 1900s.

101. Why did the United States enter World War I?

102. When did all women get the right to vote?

103. What was the Great Depression?

104. When did the Great Depression start?

105. Who was president during the Great Depression and World War II?

106. Why did the United States enter World War II?

107. Dwight Eisenhower is famous for many things. Name one.

108. Who was the United States' main rival during the Cold War?

109. During the Cold War, what was one main concern of the United States?

110. Why did the United States enter the Korean War?

111. Why did the United States enter the Vietnam War?

112. What did the civil rights movement do?

113. Martin Luther King, Jr. is famous for many things. Name one.*

114. Why did the United States enter the Persian Gulf War?

115. What major event happened on September 11, 2001 in the United States?*

116. Name one U.S. military conflict after the September 11, 2001 attacks.

117. Name one American Indian tribe in the United States.

118. Name one example of an American innovation.

119. What is the capital of the United States?

120. Where is the Statue of Liberty?

121. Why does the flag have 13 stripes?*

122. Why does the flag have 50 stars?

123. What is the name of the national anthem?

124. The Nation's first motto was "E Pluribus Unum." What does that mean?

125. What is Independence Day?

126. Name three national U.S. holidays.*

127. What is Memorial Day?

128. What is Veterans Day?

How to Overcome Test Anxiety

Just the thought of taking a test is enough to make most people a little nervous. A test is an important event that can have a long-term impact on your future, so it's important to take it seriously and it's natural to feel anxious about performing well. But just because anxiety is normal, that doesn't mean that it's helpful in test taking, or that you should simply accept it as part of your life. Anxiety can have a variety of effects. These effects can be mild, like making you feel slightly nervous, or severe, like blocking your ability to focus or remember even a simple detail.

If you experience test anxiety—whether severe or mild—it's important to know how to beat it. To discover this, first you need to understand what causes test anxiety.

Causes of Test Anxiety

While we often think of anxiety as an uncontrollable emotional state, it can actually be caused by simple, practical things. One of the most common causes of test anxiety is that a person does not feel adequately prepared for their test. This feeling can be the result of many different issues such as poor study habits or lack of organization, but the most common culprit is time management. Starting to study too late, failing to organize your study time to cover all of the material, or being distracted while you study will mean that you're not well prepared for the test. This may lead to cramming the night before, which will cause you to be physically and mentally exhausted for the test. Poor time management also contributes to feelings of stress, fear, and hopelessness as you realize you are not well prepared but don't know what to do about it.

Other times, test anxiety is not related to your preparation for the test but comes from unresolved fear. This may be a past failure on a test, or poor performance on tests in general. It may come from comparing yourself to others who seem to be performing better or from the stress of living up to expectations. Anxiety may be driven by fears of the future—how failure on this test would affect your educational and career goals. These fears are often completely irrational, but they can still negatively impact your test performance.

Review Video: 3 Reasons You Have Test Anxiety
Visit mometrix.com/academy and enter code: 428468

Elements of Test Anxiety

As mentioned earlier, test anxiety is considered to be an emotional state, but it has physical and mental components as well. Sometimes you may not even realize that you are suffering from test anxiety until you notice the physical symptoms. These can include trembling hands, rapid heartbeat, sweating, nausea, and tense muscles. Extreme anxiety may lead to fainting or vomiting. Obviously, any of these symptoms can have a negative impact on testing. It is important to recognize them as soon as they begin to occur so that you can address the problem before it damages your performance.

Review Video: 3 Ways to Tell You Have Test Anxiety
Visit mometrix.com/academy and enter code: 927847

The mental components of test anxiety include trouble focusing and inability to remember learned information. During a test, your mind is on high alert, which can help you recall information and stay focused for an extended period of time. However, anxiety interferes with your mind's natural processes, causing you to blank out, even on the questions you know well. The strain of testing during anxiety makes it difficult to stay focused, especially on a test that may take several hours. Extreme anxiety can take a huge mental toll, making it difficult not only to recall test information but even to understand the test questions or pull your thoughts together.

Review Video: How Test Anxiety Affects Memory
Visit mometrix.com/academy and enter code: 609003

Effects of Test Anxiety

Test anxiety is like a disease—if left untreated, it will get progressively worse. Anxiety leads to poor performance, and this reinforces the feelings of fear and failure, which in turn lead to poor performances on subsequent tests. It can grow from a mild nervousness to a crippling condition. If allowed to progress, test anxiety can have a big impact on your schooling, and consequently on your future.

Test anxiety can spread to other parts of your life. Anxiety on tests can become anxiety in any stressful situation, and blanking on a test can turn into panicking in a job situation. But fortunately, you don't have to let anxiety rule your testing and determine your grades. There are a number of relatively simple steps you can take to move past anxiety and function normally on a test and in the rest of life.

Review Video: How Test Anxiety Impacts Your Grades
Visit mometrix.com/academy and enter code: 939819

Physical Steps for Beating Test Anxiety

While test anxiety is a serious problem, the good news is that it can be overcome. It doesn't have to control your ability to think and remember information. While it may take time, you can begin taking steps today to beat anxiety.

Just as your first hint that you may be struggling with anxiety comes from the physical symptoms, the first step to treating it is also physical. Rest is crucial for having a clear, strong mind. If you are tired, it is much easier to give in to anxiety. But if you establish good sleep habits, your body and mind will be ready to perform optimally, without the strain of exhaustion. Additionally, sleeping well helps you to retain information better, so you're more likely to recall the answers when you see the test questions.

Getting good sleep means more than going to bed on time. It's important to allow your brain time to relax. Take study breaks from time to time so it doesn't get overworked, and don't study right before bed. Take time to rest your mind before trying to rest your body, or you may find it difficult to fall asleep.

Review Video: The Importance of Sleep for Your Brain
Visit mometrix.com/academy and enter code: 319338

Along with sleep, other aspects of physical health are important in preparing for a test. Good nutrition is vital for good brain function. Sugary foods and drinks may give a burst of energy but this burst is followed by a crash, both physically and emotionally. Instead, fuel your body with protein and vitamin-rich foods.

Also, drink plenty of water. Dehydration can lead to headaches and exhaustion, especially if your brain is already under stress from the rigors of the test. Particularly if your test is a long one, drink water during the breaks. And if possible, take an energy-boosting snack to eat between sections.

Review Video: How Diet Can Affect your Mood
Visit mometrix.com/academy and enter code: 624317

Along with sleep and diet, a third important part of physical health is exercise. Maintaining a steady workout schedule is helpful, but even taking 5-minute study breaks to walk can help get your blood pumping faster and clear your head. Exercise also releases endorphins, which contribute to a positive feeling and can help combat test anxiety.

When you nurture your physical health, you are also contributing to your mental health. If your body is healthy, your mind is much more likely to be healthy as well. So take time to rest, nourish your body with healthy food and water, and get moving as much as possible. Taking these physical steps will make you stronger and more able to take the mental steps necessary to overcome test anxiety.

Mental Steps for Beating Test Anxiety

Working on the mental side of test anxiety can be more challenging, but as with the physical side, there are clear steps you can take to overcome it. As mentioned earlier, test anxiety often stems from lack of preparation, so the obvious solution is to prepare for the test. Effective studying may be the most important weapon you have for beating test anxiety, but you can and should employ several other mental tools to combat fear.

First, boost your confidence by reminding yourself of past success—tests or projects that you aced. If you're putting as much effort into preparing for this test as you did for those, there's no reason you should expect to fail here. Work hard to prepare; then trust your preparation.

Second, surround yourself with encouraging people. It can be helpful to find a study group, but be sure that the people you're around will encourage a positive attitude. If you spend time with others who are anxious or cynical, this will only contribute to your own anxiety. Look for others who are motivated to study hard from a desire to succeed, not from a fear of failure.

Third, reward yourself. A test is physically and mentally tiring, even without anxiety, and it can be helpful to have something to look forward to. Plan an activity following the test, regardless of the outcome, such as going to a movie or getting ice cream.

When you are taking the test, if you find yourself beginning to feel anxious, remind yourself that you know the material. Visualize successfully completing the test. Then take a few deep, relaxing breaths and return to it. Work through the questions carefully but with confidence, knowing that you are capable of succeeding.

Developing a healthy mental approach to test taking will also aid in other areas of life. Test anxiety affects more than just the actual test—it can be damaging to your mental health and even contribute to depression. It's important to beat test anxiety before it becomes a problem for more than testing.

Review Video: Test Anxiety and Depression
Visit mometrix.com/academy and enter code: 904704

Study Strategy

Being prepared for the test is necessary to combat anxiety, but what does being prepared look like? You may study for hours on end and still not feel prepared. What you need is a strategy for test prep. The next few pages outline our recommended steps to help you plan out and conquer the challenge of preparation.

Step 1: Scope Out the Test

Learn everything you can about the format (multiple choice, essay, etc.) and what will be on the test. Gather any study materials, course outlines, or sample exams that may be available. Not only will this help you to prepare, but knowing what to expect can help to alleviate test anxiety.

Step 2: Map Out the Material

Look through the textbook or study guide and make note of how many chapters or sections it has. Then divide these over the time you have. For example, if a book has 15 chapters and you have five days to study, you need to cover three chapters each day. Even better, if you have the time, leave an extra day at the end for overall review after you have gone through the material in depth.

If time is limited, you may need to prioritize the material. Look through it and make note of which sections you think you already have a good grasp on, and which need review. While you are studying, skim quickly through the familiar sections and take more time on the challenging parts. Write out your plan so you don't get lost as you go. Having a written plan also helps you feel more in control of the study, so anxiety is less likely to arise from feeling overwhelmed at the amount to cover.

Step 3: Gather Your Tools

Decide what study method works best for you. Do you prefer to highlight in the book as you study and then go back over the highlighted portions? Or do you type out notes of the important information? Or is it helpful to make flashcards that you can carry with you? Assemble the pens, index cards, highlighters, post-it notes, and any other materials you may need so you won't be distracted by getting up to find things while you study.

If you're having a hard time retaining the information or organizing your notes, experiment with different methods. For example, try color-coding by subject with colored pens, highlighters, or post-it notes. If you learn better by hearing, try recording yourself reading your notes so you can listen while in the car, working out, or simply sitting at your desk. Ask a friend to quiz you from your flashcards, or try teaching someone the material to solidify it in your mind.

Step 4: Create Your Environment

It's important to avoid distractions while you study. This includes both the obvious distractions like visitors and the subtle distractions like an uncomfortable chair (or a too-comfortable couch that makes you want to fall asleep). Set up the best study environment possible: good lighting and a comfortable work area. If background music helps you focus, you may want to turn it on, but otherwise keep the room quiet. If you are using a computer to take notes, be sure you don't have any other windows open, especially applications like social media, games, or anything else that could distract you. Silence your phone and turn off notifications. Be sure to keep water close by so you stay hydrated while you study (but avoid unhealthy drinks and snacks).

Also, take into account the best time of day to study. Are you freshest first thing in the morning? Try to set aside some time then to work through the material. Is your mind clearer in the afternoon or evening? Schedule your study session then. Another method is to study at the same time of day that you will take the test, so that your brain gets used to working on the material at that time and will be ready to focus at test time.

Step 5: Study!

Once you have done all the study preparation, it's time to settle into the actual studying. Sit down, take a few moments to settle your mind so you can focus, and begin to follow your study plan. Don't give in to distractions or let yourself procrastinate. This is your time to prepare so you'll be ready to fearlessly approach the test. Make the most of the time and stay focused.

Of course, you don't want to burn out. If you study too long you may find that you're not retaining the information very well. Take regular study breaks. For example, taking five minutes out of every hour to walk briskly, breathing deeply and swinging your arms, can help your mind stay fresh.

As you get to the end of each chapter or section, it's a good idea to do a quick review. Remind yourself of what you learned and work on any difficult parts. When you feel that you've mastered the material, move on to the next part. At the end of your study session, briefly skim through your notes again.

But while review is helpful, cramming last minute is NOT. If at all possible, work ahead so that you won't need to fit all your study into the last day. Cramming overloads your brain with more information than it can process and retain, and your tired mind may struggle to recall even previously learned information when it is overwhelmed with last-minute study. Also, the urgent nature of cramming and the stress placed on your brain contribute to anxiety. You'll be more likely to go to the test feeling unprepared and having trouble thinking clearly.

So don't cram, and don't stay up late before the test, even just to review your notes at a leisurely pace. Your brain needs rest more than it needs to go over the information again. In fact, plan to finish your studies by noon or early afternoon the day before the test. Give your brain the rest of the day to relax or focus on other things, and get a good night's sleep. Then you will be fresh for the test and better able to recall what you've studied.

Step 6: Take a practice test

Many courses offer sample tests, either online or in the study materials. This is an excellent resource to check whether you have mastered the material, as well as to prepare for the test format and environment.

Check the test format ahead of time: the number of questions, the type (multiple choice, free response, etc.), and the time limit. Then create a plan for working through them. For example, if you have 30 minutes to take a 60-question test, your limit is 30 seconds per question. Spend less time on the questions you know well so that you can take more time on the difficult ones.

If you have time to take several practice tests, take the first one open book, with no time limit. Work through the questions at your own pace and make sure you fully understand them. Gradually work up to taking a test under test conditions: sit at a desk with all study materials put away and set a timer. Pace yourself to make sure you finish the test with time to spare and go back to check your answers if you have time.

After each test, check your answers. On the questions you missed, be sure you understand why you missed them. Did you misread the question (tests can use tricky wording)? Did you forget the information? Or was it something you hadn't learned? Go back and study any shaky areas that the practice tests reveal.

Taking these tests not only helps with your grade, but also aids in combating test anxiety. If you're already used to the test conditions, you're less likely to worry about it, and working through tests until you're scoring well gives you a confidence boost. Go through the practice tests until you feel comfortable, and then you can go into the test knowing that you're ready for it.

Test Tips

On test day, you should be confident, knowing that you've prepared well and are ready to answer the questions. But aside from preparation, there are several test day strategies you can employ to maximize your performance.

First, as stated before, get a good night's sleep the night before the test (and for several nights before that, if possible). Go into the test with a fresh, alert mind rather than staying up late to study.

Try not to change too much about your normal routine on the day of the test. It's important to eat a nutritious breakfast, but if you normally don't eat breakfast at all, consider eating just a protein bar. If you're a coffee drinker, go ahead and have your normal coffee. Just make sure you time it so that the caffeine doesn't wear off right in the middle of your test. Avoid sugary beverages, and drink enough water to stay hydrated but not so much that you need a restroom break 10 minutes into the test. If your test isn't first thing in the morning, consider going for a walk or doing a light workout before the test to get your blood flowing.

Allow yourself enough time to get ready, and leave for the test with plenty of time to spare so you won't have the anxiety of scrambling to arrive in time. Another reason to be early is to select a good seat. It's helpful to sit away from doors and windows, which can be distracting. Find a good seat, get out your supplies, and settle your mind before the test begins.

When the test begins, start by going over the instructions carefully, even if you already know what to expect. Make sure you avoid any careless mistakes by following the directions.

Then begin working through the questions, pacing yourself as you've practiced. If you're not sure on an answer, don't spend too much time on it, and don't let it shake your confidence. Either skip it and come back later, or eliminate as many wrong answers as possible and guess among the remaining ones. Don't dwell on these questions as you continue—put them out of your mind and focus on what lies ahead.

Be sure to read all of the answer choices, even if you're sure the first one is the right answer. Sometimes you'll find a better one if you keep reading. But don't second-guess yourself if you do immediately know the answer. Your gut instinct is usually right. Don't let test anxiety rob you of the information you know.

If you have time at the end of the test (and if the test format allows), go back and review your answers. Be cautious about changing any, since your first instinct tends to be correct, but make sure you didn't misread any of the questions or accidentally mark the wrong answer choice. Look over any you skipped and make an educated guess.

At the end, leave the test feeling confident. You've done your best, so don't waste time worrying about your performance or wishing you could change anything. Instead, celebrate the successful completion of this test. And finally, use this test to learn how to deal with anxiety even better next time.

Review Video: 5 Tips to Beat Test Anxiety
Visit mometrix.com/academy and enter code: 570656

Important Qualification

Not all anxiety is created equal. If your test anxiety is causing major issues in your life beyond the classroom or testing center, or if you are experiencing troubling physical symptoms related to your anxiety, it may be a sign of a serious physiological or psychological condition. If this sounds like your situation, we strongly encourage you to seek professional help.

Tell Us Your Story

We at Mometrix would like to extend our heartfelt thanks to you for letting us be a part of your journey. It is an honor to serve people from all walks of life, people like you, who are committed to building the best future they can for themselves.

We know that each person's situation is unique. But we also know that, whether you are a young student or a mother of four, you care about working to make your own life and the lives of those around you better.

That's why we want to hear your story.

We want to know why you're taking this test. We want to know about the trials you've gone through to get here. And we want to know about the successes you've experienced after taking and passing your test.

In addition to your story, which can be an inspiration both to us and to others, we value your feedback. We want to know both what you loved about our book and what you think we can improve on.

The team at Mometrix would be absolutely thrilled to hear from you! So please, send us an email at tellusyourstory@mometrix.com or visit us at mometrix.com/tellusyourstory.php and let's stay in touch.

Made in the USA
Las Vegas, NV
18 May 2022